To: MABS

Keep the church relevant

Reginald Davis

THE BLACK CHURCH

RELEVANT OR IRRELEVANT
IN THE 21ST CENTURY?

2/9/11

Smyth & Helwys Publishing, Inc.
6316 Peake Road
Macon, Georgia 31210-3960
1-800-747-3016
©2010 by Smyth & Helwys Publishing
All rights reserved.
Printed in the United States of America.

The paper used in this publication meets the minimum requirements of
American National Standard for Information Sciences—
Permanence of Paper for Printed Library Materials.
ANSI Z39.48–1984. (alk. paper)

Library of Congress Cataloging-in-Publication Data

Davis, Reginald F., 1964–

The Black Church: Relevant or Irrelevant in the 21st Century?
by Reginald F. Davis.
p. cm.
Includes bibliographical references and index.
ISBN 978-1-57312-557-4
(pbk. : alk. paper)
1. African American churches.
2. Black theology.
I. Title.
BR563.N4D38 2010
277.3'08308996073—dc22
2010012493

THE
BLACK
CHURCH

RELEVANT OR IRRELEVANT IN THE 21ST CENTURY?

REGINALD F. DAVIS

DEDICATION

To Johnny J. Williams of Memphis, Tennessee, for his unswerving faith and support of me while trying to help make the church relevant again. Brother Williams has demonstrated his faith in and beyond the four walls of the church. He is a constant voice crying in the wilderness for justice and fair play for all of God's children.

ACKNOWLEDGMENTS

I would like to acknowledge my father, Rev. James C. Davis, and my mother, Mrs. Annie Mae Davis, of Memphis, Tennessee, for raising me in the church and being the Christian example before me and my five brothers and one sister. I hope to be the Christian example before my children as my parents were to me. Also, I want to thank my wife, Myrlene, who has been by my side since I endeavored to do this work. Myrlene is a wonderful wife and mother to our children. Many thanks to my son, Isaac, and my daughter, Nandi, for their consistent prayers. I want to thank the whole Davis family and our friends for their prayers and support. They are too numerous to name. Last, I want to thank Smyth & Helwys for publishing this work. Their support in this process has been invaluable.

CONTENTS

PREFACE

Where justice is denied, where poverty is enforced, where ignorance prevails, and where any one class is made to feel that society is an organized conspiracy to oppress . . . and degrade [it], neither persons nor property will ever be safe . . . .

—Frederick Douglass

The Crisis

There is a crisis in black America, and I write this book with great love, admiration, and deep concern for the future of the black church. I was raised in and nurtured by the black church and am a pastor of a black church. Out of the recesses of my heart, I question the priority, operation, and direction of the black church, and seriously wonder if generations to come will have the same loyalty and respect for the black church as I do. Is liberation of the oppressed the ultimate objective of the black church, or has the black church become complicit in the ongoing oppression of black people? With the numerous black churches in America, far too many in the black community, I look on my people with the same expression Jeremiah had in the sixth century BC and make the same observation: "The harvest is past, the summer is ended, and we are not saved" (Jer 8:20).

We can certainly apply Jeremiah's statement to the plight of black America today. Physical slavery is past and the civil rights bill has been signed, and we are not saved; we are not healed; we are not organized; we are not liberated. Regardless of the small success of a few, by and large, black America is in an acute crisis. Disproportionately, we rank at the top in crime, murders, drug abuse, unemployment, incarceration, poverty, education deficiencies, and HIV/AIDS cases. All is not well with black America. Oppression of blacks in America is still a reality. The black church has not responded to this oppression adequately, and therefore the black communities continue to suffer. Amos Wilson describes the outlook of black America today despite a few gains during the 1960s black revolution of outlawing segregation, gaining the right to vote, passing fair housing legislation, and affirmative action:

> In the face of the tremendous deterioration of their quality of life—mounting unemployment, increasing poverty, crime, moral degradation; devastating miseducation and even more devastating lack of education; overwhelming drug addiction and insensate violence, homicide terror, prostitution, disease and corruption; in the face of children having children, social incivility, a youth culture whose raucous music speaks of nihilism, rape, robbery and murder, the degradation and venal hatred of black women, of everything Black…[1]

Clearly, black America is in a state of emergency, and their plight grows worse and worse. Whatever happens in America, blacks suffer a double dose of it. If America has a cold, blacks have pneumonia. If America is in a recession, blacks suffer in a depression. This is due to their economic, social, and political deficit situation in America. I understand why Albert B. Cleage Jr. stated,

> We have the same problem that Jesus had, but he was not afraid to attack the Scribes and Pharisees who were in control of the black community because he knew they were being used by the enemy. . . . Our churches also are being used to destroy our unity. Our churches are being used to block both political and economic unity. Our churches are being used against us. . . . You can't free a people as long as their leaders are taking orders from the enemy.[2]

Unless the church and its leaders break from institutions and powers that oppress God's people, and reconnect to the purpose and vision of the kingdom of God, the relevance of the black church in this twenty-first century is questionable.

Questions of Relevance

I raise searching questions for the black church. Is the black church an instrument in the hands of the enemy? Is the black church the opium of the people assisting in the disempowerment and social underdevelopment of the oppressed? Was Carter G. Woodson right when he wrote the following?

> The Negro church often fulfills a mission to the contrary of that for which it was established . . . it seems that practically all the incompetents and undesirables who have been barred from other walks of life by race preju-dice and economic difficulties have rushed into the ministry for the exploitation of the people. Honest ministers who are trying to do their duty, then, find their task made difficult by these men who stoop to prac-tically everything conceivable. Almost anybody of the lowest type may get into the Negro ministry.[3]

Is today's black church religion encouraging the embrace of oppression rather than the reduction and elimination of it? When the only institution the oppressed have created and control consistently conveys to the oppressed that God is going to take care of everything, and God can do anything but fail, the black church is helping in the process of leading the sheep to the slaughter. When predators destroy the prey, the prey should not be counseled that God will take care of everything, but rather how to resist and overcome the predator. We already know that God can do anything but fail; the issue before us is not about God but about our failure in doing the will of God on earth as it is in heaven. No people can gain liberation when they continue to leave growth and development to those who oppress them or to an agent outside the human realm. To do so is to perpetuate the miseducation and misreligion that negatively affect the black community at large.

What Is the Church's Identity?

Either the black church will stand in solidarity with the poor and the oppressed and struggle with them against oppression as Jesus did, or it will stand against them. We are either for Jesus Christ or against Jesus Christ. We cannot be for Christ and leave the destiny of the oppressed in the hands of those who oppress and exploit them through unjust systems. Christ never left the destiny of his people in the hands of oppressors, nor did he look to the oppressor to solve socioeconomic problems of the oppressed. Christ struggled with the people against oppression, and he influenced others to join him in this revolutionary movement. Nowhere do we find Christ counseling the people to accept their oppression or to wait on God to do for them what they could do for themselves. The black church puts too much emphasis on God solving problems and not enough on humans acting as co-laborers with God to solve the problems facing the black community. The black church must help black Americans understand their responsibility to believe that the kingdom of God is within them and not in anything or anyone outside themselves.

The black church must choose whom to follow and model. Will it identify with the ways of the world and model the world's systems of oppression, or will it follow Christ and identify with the kingdom of God? It must be clear about its identity. I do not believe the black church came into existence to assist the oppressed in accepting oppression, but to empower the oppressed to struggle against oppression. In order to do this, the black church and its leaders must understand how oppression works with disguises and by attacking vulnerabilities. Once the black church has an adequate understanding of oppression, then it can effectively reduce oppression and eventually get rid of it. To be relevant in the twenty-first century, the black church must attack oppression and change the theological concepts and practices that cause it to become an irrelevant institution that simply maintains status quo or does business as usual. Therefore, I write with a sense of urgency while crying in the wilderness, hoping to affect others who also love the black church and are deeply concerned about its posture and relevance in the twenty-first century. I hope the black church can learn to strategize in such a way that it becomes the black avant-garde of economic, social, and political liberation. For example, the black church must consistently address the crucial areas of black life and focus its time, resources, and action to transform these crucial areas. The black church present mission should be directed toward eradicating the root cause of black oppression, apathy, and self hatred. Once these crucial areas are properly addressed and dealt with, transformation is the by-product.

The New and Urgent Challenge Facing the Black Church

Without question, the black church is a gem. It is still the most important institution in the black community. It was and should become again the center for revolution. The black church navigated the black community through deep economic, social, and political waters that might have easily drowned hopes and dreams. It agitated for the abolition of slavery. It served as the engine of the civil rights movement and in various ways for the progress of a marginalized and exploited people. Great strides were made in the past, but these past strides cannot sustain us in our present crisis. Today, we deal with pathological situations in which human life has little to no value in many areas of black America.

Bill Cosby's assessment of the plight of black America and its youth only scratches the surface of what we truly face. Cosby said,

> People putting their clothes on backwards—isn't that a sign of something going on wrong? Aren't you paying attention? People with their hats on backwards, pants down around the crack, or are you waiting for Jesus to pull his pants up? Isn't it a sign of something when she's got her dress all the way up to the crack . . . ?"[3]

When he was criticized for airing black laundry, Cosby later responded, "Let me tell you something. Your dirty laundry gets out of school at two-thirty every day. It's cursing and calling each other nigger as they walk up and down the street. They think they're hip. They can't read; they can't write. They're laughing and giggling and they're going nowhere."[4]

In black America today, we face the extinction of family, community, culture, identity, and values as a people. What is so reprehensible is the social "quietism" of the black church. As William R. Jones points out, "quietism" is

> a refusal to reform the status quo, especially where traditional institutions and values are involved. Conformity, accommodation, and acquiescence are its distinguishing marks. Quietism becomes our operating principle if we believe that economic, social, political correction is unnecessary, impossible, or inappropriate. Corrective action is unnecessary, for instance, if we believe that some agent, other than ourselves, will handle it.[5]

Not only is there the quietism of the black church on one hand, but on the other hand is the unpreparedness of a new generation to struggle against oppression and the nihilism it produces in black America. When 70 percent of black children are born out of wedlock, many black youth drop out of high school, and the numbers of black men in prison continue to outweigh those in colleges and universities—when, in other words, our offense is failing—what kind of future defense do we have against oppression? The percentage of illiteracy among black youth, especially the incarcerated, grows higher and higher. The black church is confronted with double-digit unemployment in black America. Forty percent of black people live at or below the poverty line. There is still police brutality, racial profiling, poverty, hunger, diseases, and displacement of black people. Black-on-black crime is so grievous that black people are afraid of themselves, especially the black youth. There is an unprecedented suicide increase among black youth and an increase in other social, economic, and health issues that make the black community a nightmare and an unending holocaust.

The black community is certainly in a state of emergency. Cornel West cogently states the culture of nihilism in black America:

> To talk about the depressing statistics of unemployment, incarceration, teenage pregnancy, infant mortality, and violent crime is one thing. But to face up to the monumental eclipse of hope, the unprecedented collapse of meaning, the incredible disregard for human (especially black) life and property in much of black America is something else.[6]

To say black America is in deep spiritual, psychological, social, economic, and political trouble is an understatement. Our crisis is so critical that if we don't appropriately act against systematic oppression and the appalling apathy it produces in the oppressed, then black America will continue to disintegrate, which is a frightening and despairing reality for the future.

The black church cannot continue to deny the black crisis or treat the crisis like an elephant in the living room. No disease can be healed when people deny its existence or refuse to apply the right vaccine for the virus. The black church must face the crisis, diagnose it, and apply the right therapy to transform the present situation. Ultimately, our progress and redemption are in our hands. If we perish, we had a hand in it. If we are liberated, we had a hand in it. Our future is contingent upon our present action or inaction. Paul Loeb reminds us, "When frogs are thrown in boiling water, they jump out, but when they're placed in a pot in which the water is slowly brought to a boil, they let themselves be cooked to death. Similarly, we tolerate slow-burn crises so long as they don't touch us too directly and we have time to adjust to their effects."[7] Has the black church adjusted to the crisis facing black America in which we are cooked to death? Can the black church honestly say it struggles against the crisis, or does it continue to spiritualize the crisis by assuming God will do for us what we can do for ourselves?

Self-examination and Self-correction

The black church must do some soul searching and see to what degree it contributes to the ongoing oppression, madness, demise, and powerlessness of the black community. Second Corinthians 13:5 says, "Examine yourselves to see whether you are in the faith; test yourselves." Self-examination is crucial for the ongoing loyalty and respect of any institution, including the black church. After self-examination comes self-correction. In order to correct how it advances the maintenance of oppression, the black church must assess its beliefs and values to see if they undergird the oppression the church should resist. The unjust situation cannot correct itself. Prayer alone cannot correct it. Instead, change requires a willingness to undergo self-criticism, along with aggressive efforts to resist oppression and stem the tide of self-destructive behavior in black America.

The basic premise of this book is in the form of a challenging question to the black church: *Will the black church be relevant or irrelevant in the twenty-first century?* A relevant church struggles to correct oppression, not maintain it. Its focus is how to get rid of oppression and replace it with what promotes liberation. An irrelevant church sees the self-destructive behavior, oppression, and powerlessness of the oppressed but refuses to expose the practices of oppression that counteract the liberation of the oppressed. It also refuses to take the necessary steps to reduce oppression and eventually eradicate it. It puts resources in non-liberating activities, which adds to situations of deficit already suffered by the poor and oppressed.

To become relevant again, the black church must reorder priorities. The liberation of the black community should be first and foremost at the top of its agenda to reclaim the loyalty and respect of the black community. The church should encourage economic cooperation, job creation, education, and moral and ethical formation. It should find ways to connect disconnected generations that don't know our God or history or share our values. The black church must develop ways to resolve conflict to help eliminate the injuries and deaths of too many black men in our cities. America's prison and juvenile systems burst at the seams with black youth. Too many youth hang on the corners, forming a culture and values that further hinder them from escaping their socioeconomic predicament.

These issues stand before the black church. Will it practice business as usual, or will it become relevant by taking the necessary steps to diagnose and attack economic, social, and political oppression? By resigning from the present social order, the black church has been irrelevant for too long. If the black church elects not to become relevant again, it will be held in effigy for generations to come. The black church must reduce if not get rid of oppression, or oppression will reduce if not get rid of black people. The choice is ours, and I hope we choose to struggle against oppression and not comply with it. Decades ago, Carter G. Woodson made a cogent point about the future of the black church and community. He stated,

> The Negroes, however, will not advance far if they continue to waste their energy abusing those who misdirect and exploit them. The exploiters of the race are not so much at fault as the race itself. If Negroes persist in permitting themselves to be handled in this fashion they will always find some one at hand to impose upon them. The matter is one which rests largely with the Negroes themselves. The race will free itself from exploiters as soon as it decides to do so. No one else can accomplish this task for the race. It must plan and do for itself.[8]

The White Church

The white church, too, must do some soul searching. It has aided and abetted oppressive social institutions long enough. It must face the fact that oppressive structures were not built by the oppressed; therefore, if the white church claims to be Christian and to follow Jesus Christ, the gospel demands that it condemn racism and oppression and join the struggle in creating a freer and more just society. Lip service will not create a freer and just society. I ask the white church to struggle against oppression that affects poor people of every ethnic origin first and foremost. As Karl Barth stated, "the Church must concentrate first on the lower and lower levels of human society. The poor, the socially and economically weak and threatened, will always be the object of its primary and particular concern, and it will always insist on the State's special responsibility for these weaker members of society."[9] The white church must understand that God has always instructed his people to care for the poor and correct oppression. This is the will of God. To struggle against oppression is to struggle for the life and soul of any nation. Howard Thurman cites T. R. Glover, who writes "that the empire collapsed because the average Roman citizen had lost his sense of responsibility for the life of the empire. In other words, he had civic responsibility, but little civic responsibility. Without civic responsibility, there can be no civic character."[10]

It is often said, "Silence gives consent." The white church must come out of its deadening silence and aggressively identify with Jesus Christ, struggling to end the unjust situation of oppression and marginalization. Both the white and the black church must work together to end oppression and create a society that shows forth the kingdom of God. Walter Rauschenbusch wrote, "The Kingdom of God is humanity organized according to the will of God. . . . This involves the redemption of society from political autocracies and economic oligarchies. . . . The Church has the power to save in so far as the Kingdom of God is present in it. If the Church is not living for the Kingdom, its institutions are part of the world."[11] The church as a whole must be intentional about living for the kingdom of God and not for the institutions of the world. We must remember that in Christ, "There is neither Jew nor Greek, there is neither bond nor free, there is neither male nor female, [neither black nor white]: for we are all one in Christ Jesus" (Gal 3:28). If the white church is truly in Christ, it must struggle against oppression.

The white church should not have a different mission from the black church nor the black church from the white church. Both should "preach the gospel to the poor . . . heal the brokenhearted, preach deliverance to the captives, and recovering of sight to the blind, to set at liberty them that are bruised" (Luke 4:18). The white church has had a greater measure of freedom in society than the black church. Therefore, it should use this freedom to free others. James Cone stated, "To be free is to participate with those who are victims of oppression. Freedom, then, is more than just making decisions in light of one's individual taste. . . . Our decision affects the whole of society."[12]

I write this book to the black and white church as John wrote to the seven churches in Asia Minor. Christ spoke through the Holy Spirit to the seven churches to inform them of his commendations, expectations, and condemnation. In like manner, I write this book so the postmodern church can avoid condemnation at the Day of Judgment. Both the black and white church must stop practicing what Dietrich Bonhoeffer calls cheap grace, "the grace we bestow on ourselves . . . the preaching of forgiveness without requiring repentance, baptism without church discipline, Communion without confession, absolution without personal confession. Cheap grace is grace without discipleship, grace without the cross, grace without Jesus Christ, living and incarnate." Instead, the black and white church must return to the practice of costly grace, "the gospel which must be sought again and again, the gift which must be asked for, the door at which a man must knock. Such grace is costly because it calls us to follow . . . Jesus Christ. It is costly because it cost a man his life. . . . Above all, it is costly because it cost God the life of his Son: 'ye were bought at a price,' and what has cost God much cannot be cheap for us."[13]

Outline of Chapters

Chapter 1 assesses the importance of the black church and how it commanded the loyalty and respect of the black masses from its inception. Chapter 2 deals with why the black church is now considered the sleeping giant. In chapter 3, I outline the need for psychological conversion in black America through the purging of the miseducation/misreligion it has embraced. Chapter 4 addresses the white church and its needed role in the struggle against oppression. In chapter 5, I consider where we go from here and the kind of leadership necessary for the future of both the black and white church. Chapter 6 discusses why we need the Holy Spirit in the postmodern church. Finally, in conclusion, I investigate how the evangelicals of the nineteenth century affected their world and address how they are an example for us in making the world freer and more humane.

Notes

1. Amos Wilson, *Blueprint for Black Power: A Moral, Political, and Economic Imperative for the Twenty-first Century* (New York: Afrikan World Infosystems, 1998) 827–28.

2. Albert B. Cleage Jr., *The Black Messiah* (New Jersey: Africa World Press, Inc. 1995) 79–80.

3. Bill Cosby, Address at the NAACP on the 50th Anniversary of Brown v. Board of Education (also known as the "Pound Cake Speech"), 17 May 2004, Washington DC, http://www.americanrhetoric.com/speeches/billcosbypoundcakespeech.htm.

4. Carter G. Woodson, *Miseducation of the Negro* (Washington DC: The Associated Publishers, Inc., 1933, 1969) 68.

5. William R. Jones, "The Religious Legitimation of Counterviolence: Insights from Latin American Liberation Theology," in Lonnie D. Kliever, ed., *The Terrible Meek: Revolution and Religion in Cross-cultural Perspective* (New York: Paragon Press, 1987) 200.

6. Cornel West, *Race Matters* (New York: Vintage Books, 1993) 19.

7. Paul Rogat Loeb, *Soul of a Citizen* (New York: St. Martin's Press, 1999) 90.

8. Carter G. Woodson, *Miseducation of the Negro* (Washington DC: The Associated Publishers, Inc., 1969) 117.

9. Karl Barth, *Christian Social Teachings*, ed. George W. Forell (Minneapolis: Augsburg Publishing House, 1971) 428.

10. Howard Thurman, *The Luminous Darkness* (Richmond IN: Friends United Press, 1989) 85.

11. Walter Rauschenbusch, *Christian Social Teachings*, ed. George W. Forell (Minneapolis: Augsburg Publishing House, 1971) 377–78.

12. James Cone, *A Black Theology of Liberation* (New York: Orbis Books, 1986) 94–95.

13. Dietrich Bonhoeffer, *The Cost of Discipleship* (New York: Macmillan Publishing Company, 1963) 47–48.

Chapter 1

THE IMPORTANCE OF THE BLACK CHURCH

"Without the churches we would be in much worse shape. So we must acknowledge that they are already playing an important, even if not sufficient, role in holding back the meaninglessness and hopelessness that impinge on large numbers of black people."

—*Cornel West*

Historical Background

Regardless of the flaws, defects, and deficiencies of the black church, it is still the most important social institution in the black community. Like all institutions, the black church is not perfect, and we should point out it strengths and weaknesses to maximize its full potential. Those who criticize the black church without trying to improve upon its function and effectiveness are part of the problem. The black church is a beautiful organism within the body of Christ. It must be kept alive and free from diseases that could destroy it. It must maintain a vision to save its people from perishing. It is the only institution that black people have created and still control; indeed, "with all [its] limitations [the black church] represents the institutionalized staying power of a human community that has been under siege for close to four hundred years."[1] It promotes cultural identity, hope, survival, and liberation. Many black organizations, schools, and agencies got their start from the black church. Much of the social and political gains of black America could not have happened without the power and influence of the black church. For example, banks, credit unions, colleges, hospitals, insurance companies, newspapers, hotels, grocery stores, real estates firms, etc., all grew out of and had connection to the black church. It was and still is a powerful organization amid oppressive social and political structures. History speaks volumes of what the black church has meant to black people since its inception. Although not monolithic in its expressions of religion, the black church has created different voices that address black people's spiritual strivings and their economic, social, and political predicament.

The Break for Independence

During slavery when blacks broke away from white churches, it was their way of raising a standard by throwing off the yoke of humiliation and inferiority and establishing a church of their own that would promote and acknowledge their humanity and human potential. The break with white churches helped blacks to create a forum that would communicate their desires and deep yearnings for liberation and fulfillment. Wilmore stated, "Blacks enjoyed no real freedom or equality of ecclesiastical status in either the North or the South. It never occurred to white Christians that equality that was denied to their brothers and sisters in civil society should at least be made available to them within the church."[2] Achieving independence from the white church, blacks produced some of the greatest agitators of the unjust racial, social, and political situation. Persecuted for their biting jeremiads against racial and social injustice, these were the black preachers.

The Black Preacher

There is no question that the black preacher was the most significant influence in the lives of early black Americans. He was crucial in providing psychological and spiritual strength for the slaves. In their most difficult times, the black preacher had a word to inspire the slaves to hope against hopelessness. Amid horrifying terrorism, the black preacher served as a shepherd pleading the cause of a defenseless and despised people. Many times without permission, the black preacher preached and ministered to the slaves while in a difficult and perilous situation. It was always a situation in which the slave masters and their informants could easily view the sermons and good intentions of the black preacher as subversive. Often, the black preacher knew he was preaching on how to avoid the lash of oppression in order to minister to the needs of oppressed people. Outgunned and outnumbered, the black preacher knew he was monitored because the atmosphere was always charged with opposition to slavery. "The southern whites who observed the slave preachers at close range knew about the possible amalgam of African religion and radical Christianity. They sensed the ability of those men and women to inspire revolt and threw up the ramparts of repressive legislation and the lynch law against them."[3] One slave stated, "Back there they were harder on preachers than they were on anybody else. They thought preachers were ruining the colored people."[4] For example, Nat Turner read the Bible and the stories of how God freed the slaves. Therefore, he had a vision that God wanted him to free his people from bondage. Nat Turner the Baptist preacher led a slave revolt that sent shock waves through out the slave territories.

Black preachers provoked life in the people when society snuffed it out. The Holy Spirit was invoked as the preacher and congregation came together to express and confirm their shared experience as a way to nurture and sustain them. Whether the black preacher was giving the slaves hope for freedom and justice only in the afterlife or challenging the here and now, no other person gave direction to a rejected and despised people more than the black preacher. He helped the slaves ward off madness and self-annihilation and promoted self-worth. Howard Thurman stated that when the oppressed heard from the black preacher that they were God's children, they reached a much-needed transcendence amid frightening terrorism.

> [When] their total environment had conspired to din into their minds and spirits the corroding notion that as human beings they were of no significance, thus his one message springing full grown from the mind of God repeated in many ways a wide range of variations: "You are created in God's image. You are not slaves, you are not 'niggers'; you are God's children." Many weary, spiritually and physically exhausted slaves found new strength and power gushing up into all the reaches of their personalities. . . .[5]

The black preacher also promoted education and helped spawn other outstanding personalities to prepare the next generation to carry on the struggle for greater freedom. Wilmore stated,

> The otherworldliness of slave preaching was an interim strategy. It was the deliberate choice of the preacher to give his people something to which they could attach their emotions—something to substitute for the immediate, uncontrollable, and probably ill-fated decision to strike, then and

there, for freedom. He, therefore, gave relief from the tragedy of slavery, a modicum of comfort in the presence of the overwhelming reality of defeat and despair. Black religion may have been otherworldly, but it was not otherworldly quietistic, but otherworldly disruptive. Oppressors have never been able to relax in the presence of this kind of otherworldliness."[6]

The Black Church as Refuge

E. Franklin Frazier considered the black church "[a] nation within a nation. . . . The Negro church remained a refuge despite the fact that the Negro often accepted the disparagement of Negroes by whites and the domination of whites. . . . What mattered was the way he was treated in the church which gave him an opportunity for self-expression and status."[7] The hope of black people was centered in the black church. Although at times its liberation activities happened below the radar screen, the black church was a refuge for black people. Considering the danger that surrounded black people, the black church often quietly and sometimes not so quietly made its stance known about its opposition to slavery. Terrorism was always in the face of black people. They were very careful about their distaste for slavery. One word or incident in opposition to slavery could mean a beating or death. Then, there were situations like Nat Turner where black slaves made it known their opposition to slavery and were willing to suffer and die for it. Its "otherworldliness" may have been apparent on the surface, but there were undercurrents of radical resistance to gain liberation. Wilmore wrote, "Born in protest, tested in adversity, led by eloquent and courageous preachers, the black church was the cutting edge of the freedom movement during most of the nineteenth century. It presented itself as a living witness against the ambivalence and conservatism of most white Christians up to the Civil War."[8] Although blacks continued to experience inequality and racism in the larger society, their independent churches served as a reassurance that they were human beings made in the image and likeness of God.

The black church provided an identity for despised blacks, and what was and is most important is what blacks think of themselves. To think well of oneself is the first act against the abnegation of others. What people think of themselves determines how they will operate on behalf of their self-interest and self-determination. Consciousness of self is key to identity and liberation. Martin Luther King Jr. understood the importance of oppressed people thinking well of themselves in order to combat problems of self-hatred and powerlessness. King stated,

> The Negro will only be truly free when he reaches down to the inner depths of his own being and signs with the pen and ink of assertive self-hood his own emancipation proclamation . . . the Negro must throw off the manacles of self-abnegation and say to himself and the world: "I am somebody. I am a person. I am a man with dignity and honor."[9]

When black people think well of themselves, they demand respect while living respectably and make it known that their lives, struggles, and aspirations count. They affirm their humanity amid inhumanity and refuse to allow themselves to be abused and mistreated without resistance. However, if people believe and accept racist definitions and idiosyncrasies about themselves, they participate in the contempt. Frederick Douglass stated, "If from the cradle through life the outside world brands a class as unfit for this or that work, the character of the class will come to resemble and conform to the character described."[10] If self-esteem is absent from a people, which is one feature of oppression, they will eventually act out the character others attribute to them. The black church helped to combat self-abnegation among black people. It provided the psychological strength to aid the consciousness of the oppressed in terms of who they are before God. Howard Thurman made the following observation of how the black church combated white supremacy in terms of the cultural and psychological devaluation of black people:

> A man may be buffed about by his environment, or may be regarded as a nobody in the general community; a woman may be a nurse in a white family in which the three-year-old child in her care calls her by her first name, thus showing quite unconsciously the contempt in which she is held by his parents. When this Negro man and this Negro woman come to their church, however, for one terribly fulfilling moment they are somebody.[11]

While society barred black people from certain activities, they exercised freedom within the black church. Blacks could come to church and release their hurt and frustrations through shouts and amens. Scholars say that for the most part this was an escapist way of dealing with their oppressive environment, but nevertheless, it gave blacks the desire to live: "Going to church for blacks was never as much a matter of custom and convention as it was for whites. It was rather a necessity. The black church was the one impregnable corner of the world where consolation, unity, and mutual assistance could be found . . . ."[12] It was the one undisputed dominant institution in the black community that met the needs of the oppressed, helping them stay afloat on the restless sea of life.

The Rise of other Institutions

The black church also gave rise to other institutions within the black community. It was the advertisement agency for black businesses. The black church "[f]urnished the best opportunity for [blacks] of different social strata and various cultural groups to associate together in a thoroughgoing democratic way. . . . Up to this time, the [black] church has been one of the most outstanding channels through which gulf between the 'high' and the 'low,' the 'trained' and the 'untrained' has been bridged."[13] This bridging of the old and young, the trained and the untrained provided a sense of identity and togetherness. During this time there was no government assistance, yet the black community survived and thrived. They depended on the black church, and the black church depended on them. This union gave birth to other institutions that assisted the community, like "schools, banks, insurance companies, and low income housing," and also "an academy and an arena for political activities." Additionally, "it nurtured young talent for musical, dramatic, and artistic development."[14] This was certainly a time when the black church and community demonstrated self-help. Gayraud S. Wilmore stated,

> The black church of the nineteenth century . . . was clearer about its identity than many of us are today. . . . By every measure it was an amazing institution. . . . [T]his church converted thousands, stabilized family life . . . and provided the social, economic, political, and cultural base of the entire black community in the United States. This was a church that had a way of identifying itself which symbolized its calling to serve the broad needs of black humanity. Its identity and vocation went hand and hand.[15]

National Conventions and the Attack on White Hegemony

In the nineteenth century when independent black churches began to form national conventions such as National Negro Convention, they became an even greater threat to the sociopolitical structures of oppression. The conventions provided a national platform for black leaders to encourage the agitation of a racist and oppressive system. Black churches across America sent delegates to support the conventions and gather information as to how black people could collectively support liberation strategies. Independent black churches gave rise to Black Nationalist leaders (e.g., Richard Allen, Martin R. Delany, Alexander Crummell, Edward W. Blyden, and Henry M. Turner) who sought to reconnect blacks in America to blacks in Africa and other places in the world and who resisted white hegemony at home and abroad.[16]

The ruling class has the power to define reality and promote ideology from their privileged position. However, leaders of conventions made it clear that they would not practice social and religious quietism in the midst of white hegemony. This was a time when black leaders spoke as the prophets of old, condemning oppression and the unjust practices of the strong against the weak. They spoke truth to power without flinching and prepared to suffer the consequences. The black community pushed for change, giving black leaders the fuel and support they needed to communicate their demands. Whether through moral persuasion or the threat of using counterviolence, black people and their leaders worked together to transform the situation of oppression. There was an atmosphere of respect between the leaders and the community, and rarely did the leaders sell out communities in which they served. Black leaders did not take for granted the aspirations of the people, and served as their lightning rods against white hegemony. For example, Henry Highland Garnet, a well-respected leader of a Presbyterian Church in Troy, New York, used the convention as a platform to speak out against oppressors. His radicalism spoke directly to the situation of oppression. He believed oppressed people would never gain liberation without resistance. Thus, he urged the oppressed to resist their oppressors.

> Let your motto be resistance! Resistance! Resistance! No oppressed people have ever secured their liberty without resistance. What kind of resistance you had better make you must decide by the circumstances that surround you, and according to the suggestion of expediency. Brethren, adieu! Trust in the living God. Labor for the peace of the human race, and remember that you are FOUR MILLIONS![17]

Garnet made a case for counterviolence dictated by the circumstances of oppression. He understood that not resisting the violence produced by an oppressive context serves the maintenance needs of oppression. Garnet and others knew that in order to eliminate oppression, the oppressed must not be willing to comply with oppression. They viewed Jesus Christ as radical, and having the mind of Christ meant a willingness to sacrifice life and limb for the good of the oppressed community.

Precursors of Black Theology

Black leaders called into question the theology and interpretation of the Christian faith as espoused by whites. Leaders like Martin R. Delany and Henry McNeal Turner had the courage and audacity to reject white definitions of reality. They were precursors of black theology of liberation. Although Delany was not a clergyman, he represented, as Wilmore pointed out, the "most intellectual expression of this rudimentary black theology of the antebellum period."[18] Delany understood the need of the black church to develop its own interpretation and definition of social reality and not depend upon the dominant culture to do it for them. He understood that whoever controls the thinking of people also controls their actions. When oppressed people give up their power to interpret and define reality, they will never be liberated. Thus, Delany stated what oppressed people must boldly affirm as a consequence of their social reality:

> We are no longer slaves, believing any interpretation that our oppressors may give the word of God, for the purpose of deluding us to the more easy subjugation: but freeman, comprising some of the first minds of intelligence and rudimental qualifications, in the country. What then is the remedy, for our degradation and oppression? This appears now to be the only remaining question—the means of successful elevation in this our native land? This depends entirely upon the application of the means of Elevation.[19]

Elevation here is rising up and throwing off the manacles of oppression through the application of self-help and the determination to be liberated. The oppressed must play a role in their liberation.

Another bold leader who helped construct a black theology of liberation was Henry McNeal Turner. He had the audacity to reconstruct the color symbolism in claiming that God is black, which was an outright rebellion against classifying whiteness as beautiful and blackness as repulsive. He and Delany rejected parts of Christianity as interpreted by oppressors that did not acknowledge black peoples' humanity and redeem their situation. These leaders understood that not only did slavery grip the physical aspect of black existence, but it also dominated and controlled the psychological aspect of black life. Through attacking the interpretation of Christianity by those who claimed to be Christians, Turner laid a psychological foundation to begin the process of trying to heal the wounded psyche of an oppressed people. To change a people's condition, it is necessary first to change their consciousness. Henry McNeal Turner spoke to his critics about his radical position on the subject:

> Every race of people since time began have attempted to describe their God by words, or by paintings, or by carvings, or by any other form or figure, have conveyed the idea that the God who made them and shaped their destinies was symbolized in themselves, and why should not the Negro believe that he resembles God as much so as other people? . . . As long as we remain among the whites the Negro will believe that the devil is black and that he (the Negro) favors the devil, and that God is white and that he (the Negro) bears no resemblance to Him, and the effect of such a sentiment is contemptuous and degrading, and one-half of the Negro race will be trying to get white and the other half will spend their days trying to be white men's scullions in order to please the whites.[20]

Turner intentionally transgressed the oppressor's boundary that controlled the interpretative framework of certain categories of the Christian religion. Turner understood that as long as the oppressed operated within set boundaries, there could never be authentic liberation of the oppressed. During this period in black history, Nat Turner, Delany, Henry Turner, and others set ablaze a revolutionary religious perspective radical enough to strike fear in oppressors and potent enough to produce a pedagogy that permeated the black church, encouraging it to be an instrument in the process of rehumanization and thus helping it serve as a powerful buffer against dehumanization. One can understand why white oppressors were nervous about the revolutionary religious perspective of the black church. These steps posed a serious threat to the economic, social, and political system that produced a surplus of power for the oppressor. Although, as Wilmore pointed out,

> The majority of black preachers were not Nat Turners and were more imitative of the moralizing and peacemaking of the white clergy than was

necessary under the circumstances [, t]hey were, nevertheless, unquestion-
ably "race men." The equanimity of their spirits and the graciousness of
their language should not mislead us to assume that they were "gentlemen
of the cloth" in the grand English manner, incapable of the acrimonious
debate and passionate dissent of revolutionaries.[21]

These leaders had a vision and a religious theological perspective that
attacked the ideology of the ruling power. They wanted not only liberation
for their people but also all the safeguards that come with it.

Economic Cooperation

W. E. B. Du Bois stated, "A study of economic cooperation among Negroes
must begin with the church group."[22] Economic cooperation among blacks
was a major factor in advocating for their economic, social, and political
interests. The black church pooled its resources to buy land, build edifices,
and finance social organizations, schools, and other business ventures. This
form of cooperation kept the black church independent. The black church
understood that oppression would stand unless the oppressed cooperated
economically. Economic independence is key in building institutions that
would serve and promote the interest of the oppressed. This is why God
instructed the children of Israel in Exodus 3:21 to take silver and gold from
the Egyptians. God did not want Israel to depart from the Egyptians empty
handed. God knows that building a nation and community requires economic cooperation. Building wealth and owning goods and services are
important for the liberation and advancement of an oppressed and exploited
people. The power the black church demonstrated through economic cooperation made it an agent of economic, social, and political change. The pride
of ownership, democratic fellowship, and the spirit of freedom gave blacks a
sense of "somebodiness" that they did not feel in the larger society. Benjamin
Quarles stated, "The distinguishing mark of the Negro church was its independence from white control. Its money came from Negroes. Hence it could
speak out on such issues as slavery without fear of losing members or offending someone in the South."[23]

A Look Back at the Black Church

The Black church was relevant during the nineteenth century because not
only did it stabilize the black community but it also focused its time, energy,
and resources in uplifting the race from its downtrodden posture. Although

there were still restrictions, segregation, and discrimination, the black church confronted white oppression, invested in its community, and was at the forefront of struggling for change. It was the salt of the black community. Eloquent voices spoke out against the unjust social situation, and the individuals behind them were willing to die to redeem a people and nation. The black church was respected and supported as it moved toward the full liberation of the black community. It produced some of the greatest thinkers, writers, teachers, preachers, activists, inventors, singers, and leaders. It prepared another generation of resisters of racism and oppression. Wilmore describes the essence of the black church especially in the nineteenth century:

> We owe something inestimable to them for what they taught that the church means in terms of self-respect, meaningful participation in the affairs of the world, and in terms of an institutional base for black enterprise and culture. It was their hope to shape these gifts with all in obedience to the commandment to "go and make disciples of all nations . . . baptizing and teaching," and especially with those to whom they were bound by a common ancestry and the experience of subjugation by the white people of Europe and North America. In so doing, they demonstrated the power of their conviction that God was using the black Christians of the United States in a special way to help fulfil the promised glory of the Ethiopian people, of whom they considered themselves a privileged remnant, singing their song in a strange land.[24]

The Black Church in the Twentieth Century

The black church in the twentieth century picked up the spirit and activism of the previous century, but lost much of its radical luster due to Booker T. Washington's gradualism philosophy and the great migration of southerners to the north. Urbanization and forms of secularization put such a strain on existing black churches that the black community split into smaller sects and cults that defocused the black church from its liberation thrust. Instead, black church leaders became more or less accommodating by allowing the church to focus on non-liberating activities, ecclesiastical politics, and favors from the white power structure. This was due in part to the enactment of the Jim Crow laws, white influence in the NAACP, and the death of leaders such as Henry McNeal Tuner. The black church turned from the radicalism and nationalism of Turner to a posture of middle class accommodation and

mainline Protestantism. The plight of the lower class was no longer the primary concern of the black church. The black church became a mere social
club, and its leaders started to spiritualize oppression by preaching more
about the "hereafter" than the need for justice and freedom in the "here and
now." It went through a period of changes and adjustments that prevented it
from throwing its full weight in the quest for liberation, and it remained in
this deradicalized posture until the civil rights movement.

The civil rights movement helped the black church and its leaders regain
some loyalty and respect. Martin Luther King Jr. symbolized black freedom,
and he and other leaders broke out of the shell of gradualism and deradical-
ization. Although some leaders like Malcolm X were not Christian, they
were respected for their role in the struggle for liberation. When the civil
rights struggle changed the segregation laws of the land, the black church
stood at the center of this social change. However, after both Malcolm and
Martin died, a great hush seemed to fall over the black community.
Demonstrations and confrontations with the power structure ceased, the
aggressive struggle against racism and oppression relaxed, and the black
church slipped again into a deradicalized mode, where it largely remains
today.

Black Theology of Liberation Movement

Although James Cone and the black theology of liberation movement of the
late 1960s tried to keep alive the radical spirit of the black struggle to achieve
greater freedom and access, this movement soon became merely an academic
pursuit. James Cone acknowledges,

> We created a prophetic black theology during the 1960s that called on
> black churches to remember their liberating heritage. We reinstated the
> memory of our ancestors—their stories, songs, and sermons that subverted
> a social order that exploited and dehumanized blacks. But today we black
> theologians seem to have forgotten our own theological history. Black the-
> ology is in danger of becoming respectable in a corrupt church and in
> seminaries that favor the privileged. It is in danger of becoming nothing
> but a means of guaranteeing our professional status in white academic cir-
> cles. We have not remained on the cutting edge of history but have turned
> the revolution we started into a church social and cocktail party among
> black and white academic elites. We must remember that the vast majority
> of our people "are not fighting for ideas, for things in anyone's head. They
> are fighting to win material benefits, to live better and in peace, to see their

lives go forward, to guarantee the future of their children." . . . They are in need of new ideas about their liberation.[25]

Although black theology is relevant for our times, there is a significant disconnect of the black church leaders and black theology of liberation. Many pastors and church leaders have never heard of James Cone and black theology of liberation. Those who have heard of black theology of liberation do not preach and teach consistently about it. This is certainly a major disservice of the black church. As long as black church leaders and black theologians work exclusively of one another, black America suffers, oppression grows more rampant, and the threat of a declining democracy increases. Black America's crisis demands an aggressive and critical dialogue between the black church and black theologians. It is imperative that they both vigorously come together to develop strategies to pull the black community out of its economic, social, and political nightmare.

Nevertheless, the black church is still the cultural, economic, social, theological, and spiritual glue to hold together the process of freeing black America from its deep malaise. The black church must understand that black voices are not monolithic, and the quest for liberation requires consistent dialogue and respect for every voice. Frederick Douglass stated, "The church is the light of the world. There are individuals out of the church frequently who seize the torch of God's truth and outstrip the multitude, even the church remains behind. But the church is still the light of the world."[26] The light the black church holds must now come out from under the bushes and be lifted high to give hope once more to a people in the deep darkness of an unending midnight. The hope for the black community will not come from the government but from the black church. Black theology and the black church must never divorce. The goal is to reform the black church and put it back on the liberation track out of which it was founded. Renewal is necessary if the black church is to be relevant in the twenty-first century.

Returning to the Roots of Resistance

The black church must return to its roots of resistance by confronting oppression, institutional racism, black apathy and complacency, practicing social and economic independence, and focusing primary concern on the poor. Everything that is against black life must be confronted whether there are forces within or without. In place of empowering people, the black church provides religious comfort. Charlatans of all kinds, from prosperity preachers to self-appointed doctors and bishops, have hijacked the black church. Many of them do not understand the way oppression operates. How can the leaders of the black church apply the right therapy for the suffering community without first accurately diagnosing the cause of the people's suffering?

First, those leaders must understand the cultural crisis of the black community. Then, they must investigate the forces without and within to understand what (and who) continues to foment the crisis. If the behavior, beliefs and values of the oppressed contribute to the crisis, the goal is to transform the people by raising their consciousness about their situation. If there are external forces at work, the goal is to resist these forces and transform them into the good. In doing this there is no doubt that we shall find that the fault lies not only *without* but also *within*. Suffering people need less emotionalism and more common sense and reasoning. God does not want us to park our brains in the lot before we enter the church for worship. Emotionalism will never transform the system under which people suffer. It will not give them wisdom in addressing everyday encounters with racism and oppression.

I do not deny the importance of emotional expression in the church. Black people are emotional, and this is due in part to centuries of experience with oppression. But black people must do more than show emotion. They must aggressively act against the causes of their suffering, whether imposed from within or from without. James Cone stated, "How can we sing 'Glory Halleluiah' when our people's blood is flowing in the streets and prisons of this nation? What do we blacks have to shout about when our families are being broken and crushed by political, social, and economic forces so complex that most of us do not know what to do to resist them?"[27] To help the suffering community attack the source of the ills they suffer, leaders must have an adequate understanding of oppression. Amos Wilson describes oppression this way:

> To be oppressed is to be forced to exist not for oneself but for the other; to support one's enemies and oppose oneself and one's fellows. To be oppressed is to have one's worthiness and esteem measured in the currency of one's oppressors—to have one's value measured in coin and utility, exclusively. The oppressed are compelled to act not for their own reasons; not in order to realize their own god-given potentials or their self-defined, self-determined values; but for reasons imposed on them. Oppression requires the dissociation of the oppressed from themselves; that they deny

themselves, in service to their oppressors; that they avoid identifying with their original personality and perceive identification with it as detrimental to their survival. The rejection of their authentic selves on the part of the oppressed is a necessary preparatory step to their replacement by artificial, manipulable selves socially manufactured by their oppressors.[28]

When the leaders of the black church fail to analyze the suffering black community, they unconsciously assist the people in participating in their victimization. Oppressed people must be given the necessary tools to struggle against oppression and not taught to accept it as part of God's will. Preaching and teaching the oppressed that their situation that praise and prayer to God will alleviate their situation is not faith but superstition. Martin Luther King Jr. stated,

> We are gravely misled if we think the struggle will be won only by prayer. God, who gave us minds for thinking and bodies for working, would defeat his own purpose if he permitted us to obtain through prayer what may come through work and intelligence. Prayer is a marvelous and necessary supplement of our feeble efforts, but it is a dangerous substitute.[29]

Once the black church returns to its roots of resistance, it can again produce servant leaders like Richard Allen, Frederick Douglass, Henry McNeal Turner, Malcolm X, Martin Luther King Jr., Harriet Tubman, Fannie Lou Hammer, Rosa Parks, and others who were not afraid to stand against the forces of oppression and act on behalf of the oppressed. As Lincoln and Mamiya wrote,

> The future of the Black Church in the twenty-first century will depend as much on how it responds to the poor in its midst as to the externals of racism, the abstractions of ecumenism, or the competitive threat of a resurgent Islam. Past tradition has cast the Black Church as the proverbial "rock in a weary land"—the first and the last sure refuge of those who call it home, and all those who live in the shadow of its promises.[30]

The question is whether the black church can reclaim respect in the twenty-first century as a refuge in an effort to liberate the oppressed. One thing is sure: the black church must go beyond mere rhetoric, emotionalism, conferences, and debates. The black church must aggressively involve itself again in social and political action. It must do more than praise God with its lips; it just join God in liberating God's people through Jesus Christ our Lord.

Black church people must be doers of the word and not hearers only; they must go beyond holding meetings. Satan, the enemy of the Christian church, doesn't care about our attending church, having meetings and Bible study; he doesn't care about our national conferences and seminars. Satan cares about application. He doesn't want us to put into practice what we have learned and take action in correcting things that are out of sync with the Word of God. Satan doesn't want us to correct oppression; he doesn't want us to feed the hungry, clothe the naked, provide shelter for the homeless, and transform social and economic structures so the poor and the oppressed can increase their standard of living. He doesn't want us to carry out the mandates of the gospel. The reason Satan is working so hard against us is he knows that if we put into practice the Word of God in our individual and collective lives, his rulership is over; his influence is powerless; his throne is threatened and he would have to release our children, our marriages, and those who are held captive. Satan knows "Greater is He that is in us than he that is in the world" (1 John 4:4).

Although not perfect and certainly in need of reform, the black church is still the gathering place of oppressed people who come seeking, if nothing else, temporary release from the hurts, pains, and pressures of life. Nothing shapes oppressed people's values, beliefs, and sense of right and wrong more powerfully than the black church. It may not be all it could be in meeting the needs of the community, but it is all the oppressed have in a cruel and hostile world. Carter G. Woodson pointed out that "[t]he Negro church, although not a shadow of what it ought to be, is the great asset of the race. It is the capital that the race must invest to make a future."[32] The goal of the black church in the future is to get back to being an agent of justice, liberation, and self-help, and to model itself after the first-century church in which the people had all things in common. There was a radical distribution of resources, the needs of the people were met, and no one lacked. When basic needs are met, people are more prone to listen and to act out their responsibility in the community of faith. As long as there is a strategic plan for the empowerment of the people, more than likely they will contribute in one way or another for the uplifting of the community. The black church must strategically plan for the liberation of its people: it must encourage staying in school, teach the great contributions of black people in the world, teach financial literacy, develop businesses and industries of which black youth can use their educational skills, constantly teach moral excellence, and hold one another accountable from the homes to the schools to the churches. This village model worked before and it can work again. As it is often said, "When we fail to plan, we plan to fail."

The Challenge for the Black Church in the Twenty-first Century

In the twenty-first century, the black church cannot afford to fail the community. If it does, it will forfeit respect and loyalty. Too many people have already left the church, and many more don't see the relevance of the church in their lives. Could the following be their words?

> I was hungry
> and you formed a humanities club
> and discussed my hunger. Thank you.
> I was imprisoned
> and you crept off quietly
> to your chapel in the cellar
> and prayed for my release.
> I was naked
> and in your mind
> you debated the morality of my appearance.
> I was sick and you knelt and thanked God for your health.
> I was homeless and you preached to me
> of the spiritual shelter of the love of God.
> I was lonely
> and you left me alone
> to pray for me.
> You seem so holy;
> so close to God.
> But I'm still very hungry
> and lonely
> and cold.
>
> So where have your prayers gone?
> What have they done?
> What does it profit a man
> to page through his book of prayers
> when the rest of the world
> is crying for his?[33]

The end of the poem raises challenging questions for the black church in the twenty-first century. Christ is not interested in how many times we go to church; he is interested in us *being* the church. If our religious practices involve no more than holding meetings, conferences, annual days, and church anniversaries, then we may miss the kingdom of God. The black church must return to its heritage of resisting the forces of destruction like many of our faith ancestors did. The words of Carroll A. Watkins Ali summarize the great challenge of the black church in the twenty-first century:

> The Black church needs to come to terms with its crisis as a church and reconsider its priorities. If the choice is to champion the cause, the first priority is the survival and liberation of African Americans. Inasmuch as the Black church is the largest institution in the Black community, it is the focal point for the direction and momentum that the struggle takes. Everyone will be watching to see how the Black church responds, as we enter the twenty-first century cognizant of the fact that many African Americans live under conditions of genocidal poverty and have lost hope for the future. My prayer is that the Black church will get its houses in order and move ahead prophetically.[34]

In a similar vein, Michael Eric Dyson comments on the derailing of the black church from its traditional role in the oppressed community and challenges it to return to its prophetic role and "refocus on their mission to the downtrodden, the heavy laden, the socially outcast, the bereaved, and those imprisoned by hopelessness and despair."[35]

Notes

1. C. Eric Lincoln and Laurence H. Mamiya, *The Black Church in African American History* (Durham: Duke University Press, 1990) 398.

2. Gayraud S. Wilmore, *Black Religion and Black Radicalism: An Interpretation of the Religious History of Afro-American People* (New York: Orbis Books, 1983) 74.

3. Ibid., 82.

4. Albert J. Raboteau, *Slave Religion* (New York: Oxford University Press, 1978) 232.

5. Howard Thurman, *Deep River and the Negro Spiritual Speaks of Life and Death* (Richmond: Friends United Press, 1975) 12.

6. Wilmore, *Black Religion and Black Radicalism*, 51.

7. E. Franklin Frazier, *The Negro Church in America* (New York: Schocken Books, 1974) 51.

8. Wilmore, *Black Religion and Black Radicalism*, 95.

9. Martin Luther King Jr., *Where Do We Go from Here: Chaos or Community?* (New York: Harper and Row, 1967) 43.

10. Frederick Douglass, *Life and Times of Frederick Douglass* (New York: Macmillan Publishing Company, 1962) 474.

11. Howard Thurman, *The Luminous Darkness* (Richmond IN: Friends United Press, 1989) 21.

12. Wilmore, *Black Religion and Black Radicalism*, 76.

13. *Afro-American Religious History: A Documentary Witness*, ed. Milton C. Sernett (Durham NC: Duke University Press, 1985) 344–45.

14. Lincoln and Mamiya, *The Black Church in the African American History*, 8.

15. Gayraud S. Wilmore and James H. Cone, *Black Theology: A Documentary History, 1966–1979* (New York: Orbis Books, 1979) 244.

16. "Hegemony refers to the process by which one class exerts control of the cognitive and intellectual life of society by structural means as opposed coercive ones. Hegemony is achieved through the diffusion of certain values, attitudes, beliefs, social norms, and legal percepts that, to a greater or lesser degree, come to permeate civil society." (Hans A. Baer and Merrill Singer, *African American Religion in the Twentieth Century* [Knoxville: University of Tennessee Press/Knoxville, 1992] xx)

17. Carter G. Woodson, ed., *Negro Orators and Their Orations* (Washington DC: Associated Publishers, 1925) 155.

18. Wilmore, *Black Religion and Black Radicalism*, 109.

19. Cited in ibid., 111.

20. Cited in ibid., 125.

21. Ibid., 95.

22. Cited in E. Franklin Frazier, *The Negro Church in America*, 40.

23. Benjamin Quarles, *Black Abolitionists* (New York: Oxford University Press, 1969) 82.

24. Wilmore, *Black Religion and Black Radicalism*, 134.

25. James H. Cone, *For My People: Black Theology and the Black Church* (New York: Orbis Books, 1984) 198–99. Cone quotes Amilcar Cabral, leader of African nationalist movements in Guinea-Bissan and Cape Verde.

26. Frederick Douglass, "Brilliant Thoughts and Important Truth: A Speech of Frederick Douglass," Ohio, 1852, ed. Larry Gara, professor of history and government at Wilmington College, p. 5.

27. Cone, *For My People*, 197.

28. Amos N. Wilson, *The Falsification of African Consciousness* (New York: Afrikan World InfoSystems, 1993) 132–33.

29. Martin Luther King Jr., *Strength to Love* (Philadelphia: Fortress Press, 1963) 131–32.

30. Lincoln and Mamiya, *The Black Church in African American History*, 404.

31. James H. Cone, *Black Theology and Black Power* (New York: Orbis Books, 1997) 111.

32. Carter G. Woodson, *Miseducation of the Negro* (Washington DC: Associated Publishers, Inc., 1969) 52–53.

33. Cited from James Cone, *Speaking the Truth* (New York: Orbis Books, 1999) 113.

34. Carroll A. Watkins Ali, *Survival & Liberation: Pastoral Theology in African American Context* (St. Louis: Chalice Press, 1999) 153.

35. Michael Eric Dyson, *Can You Hear Me Now?* (New York: Basic Civitas Books, 2009) 21–22.

Discussion Questions

1. Consider your experience with the black church. Do you agree that it is, as the author states, "still the most important social institution in the black community"? If so, why? If not, what has taken its place?

_____

_____

_____

_____

2. Do you or members of your family have personal stories about how the black church has affected you? Have you or people you know ever considered it a refuge? In what ways did it perform this function? In general, do you think it still performs this function for people today?

_____

_____

_____

_____

3. The author states that Booker T. Washington's "gradualism philosophy," along with the "great migration of southerners to the north," lessened the radical nature of the black church. Rather than continuing to push for the liberation of black people from societal constraints, the church focused inward, becoming more of a "social club." What are the positive aspects of this purpose of the church? In the twenty-first century, how important do you think it is for the black church to continue to strive for equality?

_____

_____

_____

_____

4. How can your particular church, whether made up of mostly black members or members of other races, diagnose the current problems facing African Americans?

_____

_____

_____

_____

5. The author writes that "the black church must go beyond mere rhetoric, emotionalism, conferences, and debates." Do you think these are still necessary? Do you think your church needs to get involved in social and political action? Why? If so, what practical steps can you take to do so?

_____

_____

_____

_____

Chapter 2

THE SLEEPING GIANT
AMID A PEOPLE IN CRISIS

*"One of the great liabilities of life is that all too many
people find themselves living amid a great period of
social change and yet they fail to develop the new attitudes, the new mental responses that the new situation
demands. They end up sleeping through a revolution.*
                              —Martin Luther King Jr.

While the Black Church Sleeps

Legend says Napoleon once pointed to a map of China and said, "There lies
a sleeping giant. If it ever wakes up, it will be unstoppable."[1] When we look
at the black church, we can say what Napoleon said about China. "There lies
a sleeping giant." While the black church sleeps, black America is torn apart
by violence, scarcity of resources, unemployment, meaninglessness, miseducation, and health-damaging conditions like hopelessness and apathy. As the
economic gap for black America widens, more prisons are built and filled
with a disproportionate number of black people. The black underclass feels
the pain of isolation and alienation, and, according to Ellis Cose, the rage
among the privileged class mounts:

> Despite its very evident prosperity, much of America's black middle class is
> in excruciating pain. And that distress—although most of the country does

not see it—illuminates a serious American problem: the problem of the broken covenant, of the pact ensuring that if you work hard, get a good education, and play by the rules, you will be allowed to advance and achieve to the limits of your ability.[2]

Many believe the dream that Martin Luther King Jr. articulated is progressively showing signs of Malcolm X's nightmare. Fear and uncertainty in black America have reached disastrous levels. Self-sabotage and self-destruction are all too common in the black community. The black church sleeps through one of the most critical times in human history, forfeiting a great opportunity to bring about positive and lasting change to a people in crisis.

Cain Hope Felder wrote about the profound slumber of black America in general and the black church in particular, comparing them to the "jungle sloth" from a story he read in high school. The sloth's "sluggish routine included little more than eating, moving about upside down, or just hanging in trees, always seeking some comfortable place to rest and sleep . . . sleep . . . sleep!" Felder likens many black communities to

> colonies of jungle sloths—complacent, selfish, toothless, and complaining, whether seeming "masters" or manifest victims of endless excuses at a time when such excuses only foster further socioeconomic, political, and spiritual erosion. . . . Many in the Black community have in varied ways fallen back to sleep amid the galvanizing shocks and cries of the modern era. Past visions of creativity, achievement, and solidarity are on the wane, and too many in our time find a woeful kinship with the jungle sloth![3]

I am not sure how the black church can remain relevant in a state of profound unconsciousness. Many people come to church Sunday after Sunday to have their emotional thirst quenched, but they still suffer psychologically, economically, and socially. Emotional satisfaction lasts only so long before it becomes distress and bitterness. Frederick Douglass discovered years ago that the church has "substituted religion for humanity. We have substituted a form of Godliness, an outside show for the real thing itself. We have houses built for the worship of God, which are regarded as too sacred to plead the cause of the downtrodden million in them."[4] These days the black church is addicted to religiosity instead of liberation. It spends more time, energy, and resources on non-liberating activities like church programs, annual days, conferences, and conventions than on liberating the community from economic, social, and political oppression. Martin Luther King Jr. stated, "We must never let it be said that we spend more for the evanescent and ephemeral than for the eternal values of freedom and justice."[5] Due to its unconsciousness, the priority of the black church is not where it ought to be.

Comatose

What will it take to wake us up? The custodians of the American judicial system have neither the interest nor the willingness to stop the oppressive recycling described by Amos Wilson, who wrote about the system taking the weak and processing them "so that everyone else gets a piece of them": the cop, the lawyer, the court officers, the correction officers, and the parole officer.[6]

It appears that the struggle of the black community has not awakened the sleeping giant; thus, it seems that the black church must have slipped into a coma. The black crisis in America speaks too loudly for the black church to remain asleep. If the gunshots of the black community; the cries of mothers who have lost their sons and daughters to drugs and violence; the more than two million blacks in prison, 90 percent of whom are illiterate; the 70 percent of black children born out of wedlock; the double-digit unemployment rate in the black community; the AIDS epidemic at home and in Africa; Hurricane Katrina's displacement of thousands of black people; and the molestation and murder of children in the black community haven't awakened the church, then we must conclude that the black church lies in a coma, a state of deep and prolonged unconsciousness. There is no other way it could remain asleep amid the chaos in black America. We must take steps to awaken the black church. We dream while sleeping. The dream can be pleasant or a nightmare. Martin Luther King Jr.'s dream of a liberated people cannot happen unless we wake up and make the dream a reality; otherwise, Malcolm X's nightmare will be our reality:

> No, I'm not an American. I'm one of the 22 million black people who are victims of Americanism. One of the . . . victims of democracy, nothing but disguised hypocrisy. So, I'm not standing here speaking to you as an American, or a patriot, or a flag-saluter, or a flag-waver-no, not I! I'm speaking as a victim of this American system. And I see America through the eyes of the victim. I don't see any American dream; I see an American nightmare![7]

Trumpet Blast

In ancient times, God instructed the prophet Ezekiel to blow his trumpet to warn the people of God's impending judgment. As God long ago instructed the prophet to alert the people, God today calls the conscious leaders of the black church to blow the trumpet to wake up the sleeping giant and call attention to the community's crisis. Few enjoy pointing out the wrongs of their fellow countrymen. Few prefer to carry bad news or blow a trumpet while others sleep comfortably. Few wish to be labeled a troublemaker. Few want to disturb rather than comfort. But there comes a time when we must accept the labor and burden of curing the soul. There comes a time when we must disturb, a time when we must "comfort the afflicted and afflict the comfortable." It is not something we relish, but woe unto us if we don't speak out. Although it is dangerous and life threatening to stand and tell the truth in a climate of religious hypocrisy, political lies, and social deceit, nevertheless, we who are awake and conscious must do so if we are to save the black community from self-destruction. James Cone wrote, "Preaching the gospel, doing Christian theology, and speaking the truth are interrelated, and neither can be correctly understood apart from liberation struggles of the poor and marginalized."[8] If the church is not for Christ, it is against Christ, and we cannot be for Christ and neglect the poor and the oppressed.

God's prophets were often compelled to speak the truth, and they called into question the practices and dealings of the people. The persistent theme in Israelite prophecy is God's concern for the lack of economic, social, and political justice for the marginalized of society. The Hebrew prophets made it clear that God's anger is riled when the poor have no defense and when they are constant victims of injustice. The prophets show us that God is a God of liberation. If the black church prefers ease and comfort to arming itself with the gospel of liberation against oppression, then there is nothing the prophet can do when the crisis produces destruction. One thing is certain, however: if the leaders of the postmodern church fail to warn those who control the social system, the blood of the people will be on the hands of the leaders. God gives the prophet a warning in Ezekiel 33:6: "But, if the watchman see the sword come, and blow not the trumpet, and the people be not warned; if the sword come, and take any person from among them, he is taken away in his iniquity; but his blood will I require at the watchman's hand." God expects the church and its leaders to warn those in power about God's displeasure with injustice, and when the church and its leaders fail to do this, God will hold the church and its leaders responsible. Speaking out against evil and injustice is a mandate that the church cannot circumvent. The messages the prophets delivered were often unpopular and not politically correct, but they got to the heart of the people's problem.

No Resistance

The postmodern black church has accepted oppression with little to no resistance, allowing the ongoing wrongs against the poor and undeveloped nations of the world without aggressive protest. Sleep produced apathy that perpetuates the reign of oppression in the black community. Amos Wilson stated, "Apathy in subordinated Afrikans provides White supremacy its strongest bulwark against defeat. The greatest struggle of oppressed Afrikans is not against their White oppressors but against their own apathy."[9] It is well documented that God is against the church for allowing oppression over liberation, profit over human life, and programs over ministries that do not set captives free. Amid a racist social system, the sleeping church sits in silence while the disintegration of the black community continues to spin out of control. Without the cooperation of the church and community, the prospects for a better day are bleak. Unless the church resists forces of destruction and turns its "audience into an army and transform[s] spectators into participants," the black community will continue to experience alienation and disintegration.[10]

Paul Tillich blamed the ruling group for a nation's atrocities. "But all individuals in a nation are responsible for the existence of the ruling group," he wrote. "Not many individuals in Germany are directly guilty of the Nazi atrocities. But all of them are responsible for the acceptance of a government which was willing and able to do such things."[11] As long as the black church refuses to resist evil and injustice, the unjust system will continue to grind the people of God to dust. If the people awaken at the rousing trumpet blast of truth only to fall asleep again, they do this at their own peril. If they are destroyed, they cannot blame anyone but themselves, for they received ample warning.

Our Collective Goal

Our collective goal as pastors, theologians, and Christian educators is to wake up the sleeping giant. The black church must be part of the solution, not the problem. In order to transform black America's present situation, the black church must wake up, stand up, and step up to bring the community out of its deep and disturbing malaise. The black church can never truly be free until the community it serves is set free. The destiny of the two is tied together. The community affects the life of the church, and the church affects the life of the community. The two must work together to transform the present situation. This requires renewal in the black church, a reordering of priorities to serve the suffering masses so that the black church is relevant in the twenty-first century.

For example, black churches like Trinity United Church of Christ in Chicago, New Birth in Georgia, Abyssinia Baptist church in New York City, Crenshaw Christian Center in California, New Light Christian Center in Texas, and many more are operating programs to feed the hungry, shelter the homeless, educate the disadvantaged; they are giving financial support to jumpstart black businesses, holding literacy programs, and creating an atmosphere and space for youth activities. Although they are few in number compared to the number of black churches across the country, these churches are models of relevancy in one way or another for the twenty-first century. The goal is to get more churches involve in meeting the needs of the community for its liberation. When the black church commits itself to the liberation of the community and empowers people by helping them take charge of their lives for the creation of a new humanity, then the black church becomes relevant once again.

To overlook the liberation of a suffering people by highlighting other interests like annual days, church anniversaries, building edifices, and conferences, etc., is to make religion the opiate of the people. Since Jesus Christ is the head and master of the church, the church is his servant in society. As Cone wrote, "Being a servant of Jesus involves more than meeting together every Sunday for worship and other liturgical gatherings. . . . Servanthood includes a political component that thrusts a local congregation in society, where it must take sides with the poor. Servanthood is a call to action that commits one to struggle for the poor."[12] It is a call to struggle against institutional structures that keep the poor handicapped and hopeless. The church must develop a liberating mind by seeing life from the same perspective as Christ saw it. Jesus Christ saw the poor, the oppressed, the hungry, the blind, the lame, the outcast of society and made them his primary concern. With a liberating mind, the church can work to liberate the oppressed and proclaim the kingdom of God.

Questions and Concerns about Integration

Without question, the black church was at the center of helping black America desegregate during the 1960s. Today, black America is an allegedly integrated people but surely not an independent people. Many of us thought integration was the social, economic, and political salvation of the black community. As we look back and analyze integration, though, some question its effectiveness. Did integration help or hurt us as a people? Was integration the panacea for economic, social, and political oppression? Are some of the staggering statistics facing black people due in part to integration? The questions of integration are not an indictment against Martin Luther King Jr. and those who struggled to better the plight of black America. However, these questions are raised in light of deteriorating conditions, the high percentage of high school dropouts, and the unacceptable level of underachievement of too many of our black youth in the post-civil rights struggle.

We are still sleeping if we think we have fully integrated in our American society. A social change has been made, but change does not mean a correction takes place. It is possible to change something without correcting it. For instance, a house with structural problems can be beautified to give the appearance of a sound building. Whatever is done to beautify the house is a change, but the house is not actually sound without a structural correction. The social structures in America have made a change, but they are not corrected. There is still inequality in power, education, medical care, and other areas. Until it is verified that black people have fully integrated by holding equal power and serving in the decision-making process that creates polices directly affecting the lives of black people, the situation of integration is questionable. True integration is when two equal powers come together. The cultural ideals of both must be included, but when one cultural ideal is advanced at the expense of everything that conforms to it, assimilation, not integration, takes place.[13]

The power of black people is not equal to that of white people. The civil rights struggle was actually an exercise in assimilation. Assimilation absorbs the culture, character, and uniqueness of a people and places them in an unequal position within the power structure to enhance the survival and well-being of the dominant group. It is called integration, but it is really assimilation. Black America must understand that racism, like oppression, is an exercise in power, and until blacks have equal power, the problem of racism and oppression remains. Paulo Freire wrote, "The solution is not to 'integrate' [the oppressed] into the structure of oppression, but to transform that structure so [the oppressed] can become 'beings' for themselves."[14] Additionally, Amos Wilson made a cogent observation about integration:

> We are hanging by a thin thread. The more "integrated" we become, the weaker we become: the more dependent we become. One day when we think we've got it made at the mint, when we are "holding hands with little Black girls and little White girls" — the switch will fall. And then we find out that we are left completely in the open not having prepared at all to deal with the situation. The Jews learned a serious lesson about that: we can be in the universities; we can create an Einstein: we can make great contributions to this society but that may not keep us from going to the oven.[15]

Progression but No Possession

Many argue that blacks have made progress, and I don't disagree with this assessment. We have black mayors, governors, senators, congresspersons, and CEOs of major corporations. We have civil rights and voting rights. While I cannot deny the progress of black America, black America needs to wake up and understand that we have not achieved total liberation. We have not possessed economic, social, and political power in such a way to become power brokers in the American economy. Having positions and titles doesn't mean black people are liberated. Unless a people possess power, they cannot counter the power that rules over them and turns against them. They are at a dangerous disadvantage. Those who think black America has arrived and has integrated, and that there is no longer a need for social, economic, and political struggle, Must consider questions like these Wilson proposes:

> Who has control of your food? Who has control of your electricity? Who has control of your water? Of your jobs? . . . What would happen if these [places] we live in today are surrounded by a force that blocks the food and the water, cuts off the electricity and the other things? What kind of situation would we be in? . . . Therefore, if we wish to change this situation (i.e., the conditions under which we live), then we must change the power relationships. If we are to prevent ourselves from being created by another people and are to engage in the act of self-creation, then we must change the power relations.[16]

Being at the mercy of another group does not mean liberation and equality. Black America must start to depend on itself and harness power itself; otherwise, another people will always exercise power over them. This is a perilous position for black people. The African holocaust and Nazis Germany are distinguishing reminders of what can happen to a people in subjugation.

Economic Infrastructure

To change the power relationship, black America must develop its own economic infrastructure. Blacks cannot achieve this by building a church on every corner. We have too many churches and not enough businesses. As Ernest M. Fountain reminded us, "for profit businesses started non-profit businesses for the purpose of reducing their tax burden in an effort to address the social ills of society."[17] Since churches are classified as non-profit organizations, black America cannot create an economic infrastructure by having churches, all non-profits, and no businesses, or for-profits. The black community needs more businesses than churches to change the conditions under which its people live. Ali asks, "Could it be that we have somehow lost sight of the people for the church building we feel so compelled to build? Could it be that these structures, some so massive, are blocking our view of the mission field right outside the church doors? . . . The black church is in crisis, as it fails to adequately address the collective survival and liberation issues of Black America."[18]

The black church must wake up and understand how critical economic power is to the liberation of the community. Too much of the resources of the black church and community are wasted on non-liberating ventures. The great outflow of black dollars impoverishes the black community. The black community unemployment rate is in the double digits, and this is part of not having an economic infrastructure. Because there is no employment in the black community, crime and hopelessness are played out in the streets of our cities. Black-on-black crime is a grievous example of people preying on themselves just to survive, and until the black church understands how economy works for job creation in the black community, blacks will continue to fill the morgues of our cities. It is heartrending to know that black America has a buying power in the billions of dollars, but the black community is not benefiting from those billions. In an editorial, Lamarr Brown stated,

The overall consumerism of Blacks in America is enough to run a third world country; yet, Blacks in America have no means of production, control, or distribution of the majority of the goods and services that are needed in the Black community. . . . Several major areas of Black consumerism are targeted by other ethnic groups who come to America, receive government loans to purchase businesses in our Black neighborhoods, and at the end of the day take the money away without any reinvestments in our Black communities.[19]

No one but the black community can stop this situation. Carter G. Woodson wondered, "Why should the Negro wait for some one from without to urge him to self-assertion when he sees himself robbed by his employer, defrauded by his merchant, and hushed up by government agents of injustice?"[20] Foreigners who come into the black community and set up businesses are taking advantage of economic opportunities that are the same for blacks. Until black America commits to loving and supporting itself, others will always impose upon blacks, exploit them, and manipulate them.

Black Relational Problems

Black America must wake up to see that the problem is in themselves. The core problem with black America is a relational issue. Many black people don't relate well with one another, and thus they cannot lift themselves from the quicksand of hopelessness to the solid rock of possibility. Blacks often are socialized not to trust themselves, and when a people don't trust themselves, it doesn't matter how much money they have; they will not rise economically. Black America is not suffering from a lack of money. According to the Selig Center for Economic Growth, black America's buying power will rise from

> 318 billion in 1990 to 921 billion in 2008, up by 189 percent in eighteen years—a compound annual growth rate of 6.1 percent. This overall percentage gain outstrips the 128 percent increase in white buying power and the 148 percent increase in total buying (all races combined). In 2008, the nation's share of total buying power that is black will be 8.7 percent, up from 8.4 percent in 2003 and up from 7.4 percent in 1990. Nationally, African Americans consumers account for almost nine cents out of every dollar that is spent.[21]

The problem is not a lack of money among black Americans. The problem is that black Americans do not relate well with each other, and therefore have not built an economic infrastructure or a base to benefit from the buying power they possess.

Amos Wilson stated, "A system involves the systematic and organized utilization of money; a systematized utilization and distribution of money. Without the pattern, without the system, without the organization, one does not have an economy."[22] Black America needs an economic infrastructure that is predicated upon the systematic way blacks choose to relate to one another. As long as we as blacks continue to hate each other, undermine each other, not work together, and not organize together, "[w]e can have money and still be poor, have money and be robbed, which is what we are."[23] Our social, political, and economic empowerment begins with our love for one another and how we choose to relate to each other. Blacks operate individually, while other groups think and operate collectively, and this is why we are stuck in the cycle of depending on others to provide jobs, goods, and services. Blacks must realize that their disunity is somebody else's capital gain. Black America has not become fully conscious of having an economic foundation before trying to build a political base. Without an economic foundation, the interest of the black community is always in jeopardy.

It doesn't matter how many black mayors, politicians, or elected officials serve across this nation; without an economic base, the plight of black America will continue to worsen. Martin Luther King Jr. stated, "The majority of Negro political leaders do not ascend to prominence on the shoulders of mass support . . . most are selected by white leadership, elevated to position, supplied with resources and inevitably subjected to white control."[24] The responsibility for controlling the black community and creating an economic base to participate in power and the decision-making process rests on the shoulders of black America. "No people can be truly free whose liberty, jobs, well being, and future is dependant upon others," wrote Frederick Douglass, "and they don't have the means in their own hands for guarding, protecting, defending, and maintaining that liberty."[25]

The black church must wake up and understand that economics drives the world. We can have religion and education and still starve. As Booker T. Washington said, "At the bottom of education, at the bottom of politics, even at the bottom of religion, there must be for our race economic independence."[26] Unless we learn the importance of economics in the survival and liberation of a people, we may not exist in the near future, and if we do exist, we shall be at the economic mercy of others as we are today. If the black church doesn't wake up to recognize the crisis of the black community

and understand how economics works in the global economy, then disintegration, welfare dependency, unemployment, crime, and death shall
continue to overcome us. We must remember that the black church is still
the institution of empowerment in the black community. To empower is to
help people get in touch with the power that is theirs—to help them identify
their power, claim their power, and/or to recover power that has been taken
from them," wrote Carroll Ali.[27] There is nothing wrong with having power;
indeed, power is essential for survival. The concern is how to use power once
we have it.

Political Involvement

To empower the people, the black church cannot resist being politically
involved. We must honor the sacrifices of those who advanced liberation for
the black church. Legislation must secure whatever is done to raise people's
level of humanity. Martin Luther King Jr. stated,

> There are always those individuals who argue that legislation, court orders,
> and executive decrees from the federal government are ineffective because
> they cannot change the heart. They contend that you cannot legislate
> morals. It may be true that morality cannot be legislated, but behavior can
> be regulated. The law may not change the heart, but it can restrain the
> heartless. It will take education and religion to change bad internal atti-
> tudes, but legislation and court orders can control the external effects of
> bad internal attitudes.[28]

We need to be engaged in the political process. The mission of the church is
to transform every segment of society. People must be empowered not only
by economics but also by legislation that protects their empowerment. Peter
Hinchliff made this cogent statement: "Politics is about power . . . in the
sense of the ability to compel obedience: to the party or people in office, to
the public servants who administer government, to the generality of citizens
who desire to protect by law their persons or property."[29]

  It is my hope that the black church awakens to see that it is our
Christian duty to help shape a just and moral society, and we cannot do this
by being apolitical. If the black church is to be relevant in the twenty-first
century, its people cannot opt out of politics. They must get involved to help
create public policies that are just and fair not only for the black community
but for all people. The time has come for sideline spectators to become

involved participants in transforming society. We must wake up before immorality takes us over and we find ourselves again in exile in our own homeland. Not only will black Americans find themselves in exile, but, as James Cone stated, "If African-American churches do not wake up and seriously take note of the signs of the times in the world, they will find themselves oppressors of their brothers and sisters in the Third World."[30] Our position as blacks in America greatly affects the position of blacks abroad.

The Work of the Kingdom

The work of God's kingdom must move beyond the narrow confines of our stained-glass windows. We cannot accomplish anything for the kingdom of God by sleeping and retreating into our private devotions while our world spins out of control. Christianity was never meant to be a private affair; it is a public witness. William Barclay wrote,

> Christianity was never meant to withdraw a man from life; it was meant to equip him better for life. Christianity does not offer us release from problems; it offers us a way to solve our problems. Christianity does not offer us an easy peace; it offers us a triumphant warfare. Christianity does not offer us a life in which troubles are escaped and evaded; it offers us a life in which troubles are faced and conquered. . . . The Christian must never desire to abandon the world; he must always desire to win the world.[31]

Notes

1. Cited in Rick Warren, *The Purpose Driven Church* (Grand Rapids MI: Zondervan, 1995) 365.

2. Ellis Cose, *The Rage of a Privileged Class* (New York: HarperCollins Publishers, Inc., 1993) 1.

3. Cain Hope Felder, *Troubling Biblical Waters* (New York: Orbis Books, 1989) 92–93.

4. In Philip S. Foner, ed., *The Life and Writings of Frederick Douglass*, vol. 2 (New York: International Publishers, 1950–1975) 180.

5. Martin Luther King Jr., *A Testament of Hope*, ed. James Melvin Washington (San Francisco: Harper & Row, Publishers, 1986) 143.

6. Amos N. Wilson, *Awakening the Natural Genius of Black Children* (New York: Afrikan World InfoSystems, 1991) 7.

7. *Malcolm X Speaks*, ed. George Breitman (New York: Grove Press, 1965) 26.

8. James H. Cone, *Speaking the Truth* (New York: Orbis Books, 1999) v.

9. Amos N. Wilson, *The Falsification of Afrikan Consciousness* (New York: Afrikan World InfoSystems, 1993) 132.

10. Warren, *The Purpose Driven Church*, 367.

11. Cited in George W. Forell, *Christian Social Teaching* (Minneapolis: Augsburg Publishing House, 1966) 408.

12. Cone, *Speaking the Truth*, 124.

13. William R. Jones, "The Arts in the Community: Toward a Deeper Understanding of Black Aesthetics," unpublished manuscript, p. 9.

14. Paulo Freire, *Pedagogy of the Oppressed* (New York: Continuum Publishing Company, 1999) 55.

15. Wilson, *Awakening the Natural Genius of Black Children*, 5.

16. Wilson, *The Falsification of Afrikan Consciousness,* 16–17.

17. Ernest M. Fountain, *To Achieve the American Dream* (Las Vegas: Fountain Financial Services LLC, 2002) 48.

18. Carroll A. Watkins Ali, *Survival and Liberation: Pastoral Theology in African American Context* (St. Louis: Chalice Press, 1999) 148.

19. Lamarr Brown, "Is There an Economic War on Black America?" *New Journal & Guide*, Norfolk VA, 26 October 2005.

20. Carter G. Woodson, *Miseducation of the Negro* (Washington DC: The Associated Publishers, Inc., 1969) 187–88.

21. Jeffrey M. Humphreys, "The Multicultural Economy 2003: America's Minority Buying Power," *Georgia Business and Economic Conditions* 63/2 (second quarter 2003): 3.

22. Wilson, *The Falsification of Afrikan Consciousness*, 44.

23. Ibid., 45.

24. King, *A Testament of Hope*, 605.

25. Frederick Douglass, *The Life and Times of Frederick Douglass* (New York: Pathway Press, 1941) 213.

26. *Famous Black Quotations*, selected and compiled by Janet Cheatham Bell (Chicago: Sabayt Publications, 1986) 45.

27. Ali, *Survival and Liberation*, 139.

28. King Jr., *A Testament of Hope*, 100–101.

29. Peter Hinchliff, *Holiness and Politics* (Grand Rapids MI: William B. Eerdmans Publishing Company, 1982) 62.

30. James H. Cone, *For My People: Black Theology and the Black Church* (New York: Orbis Books, 1984) 141.

31. William Barclay, *The Gospel of John*, vol.2 (Philadelphia: The Westminster Press, 1956) 252.

Discussion Questions

1. In this chapter, the author describes the black church as a "sleeping giant." He quotes Frederick Douglass, who wrote these words several decades ago: "We have houses built for the worship of God, which are regarded as too sacred to plead the cause of the downtrodden million in them." In what ways does this statement still apply to American churches in general? How does it specifically apply to the black church?

_____

_____

_____

_____

2. Look through your Bible for passages about liberation, such as the story of the exodus from Egypt (Exod 12ff.), the statement in Galatians about unity in the faith (Gal 3:26-28), and the assertion of Christ's freedom in John 8:36. Also consider passages about social justice, such as the parable of sheep and goats in Matthew 25 and numerous instructions about caring for the poor as recorded in the Gospels. How are churches today living out these mandates? How are they failing?

_____

_____

_____

_____

3. In your opinion, have black Americans truly integrated into society, or have they merely assimilated into America's social structures?

_____

_____

_____

_____

4. Why might the way blacks relate to each other be part of the reason for their continued oppression? In your personal experience, do you notice distrust among African Americans?

_____

_____

_____

_____

5. The author asserts that economic power and political involvement are critical to the liberation of black people. First, what would liberation mean for blacks? Second, what is the role of the black church in empowering African Americans both economically and politically?

_____

_____

_____

_____

Chapter 3

BLACK AMERICA'S NEED FOR A PSYCHOLOGICAL CONVERSION

"We are convinced that recognizing the origin and the continued manifestation of this psychological bondage is the start of a self-healing process which we as a people must engage in both individually and collectively."
—Naim Akbar, Ph.D.

Black Americans Must Change the Way They Think

There is no doubt about it that if the plight of black Americans is to be transformed, then the black church and community must change the way they think. Changing a people's condition requires first changing their consciousness. Black America must undergo a psychological conversion. Black Americans have grown to believe the negative and distorted images of themselves, effectively participating in their own oppression. In struggling to fit within the standards of the dominant culture, they end up negating their own history, culture, and self-worth. As W. E. B. Du Bois articulated years ago, black America battles a double consciousness.

The history of the American Negro is the history of this strife—this longing to attain self-conscious manhood, to merge his double self into a better and truer self. . . . He simply wishes to make it possible for a man to be both a Negro and an American, without being cursed and spat upon by his fellows, without having the doors of Opportunity closed roughly in his face . . . it is a peculiar sensation, this double consciousness, this sense of always looking at one's self through the eyes of others, of measuring one's soul by the tape of a world that looks on in amused contempt and pity. One ever feels his twoness—an American, a Negro; two souls, two thoughts, two unreconciled strivings; two warring ideals in one dark body, whose dogged strength alone keeps it from being torn sunder."[1]

Du Bois describes a split psyche in black Americans that keeps them at war with themselves and others.

Clearly, black Americans suffer from psychological nihilism. Self-hatred and self-sabotage arise from a consciousness shaped by oppression and negative cultural images. Trying to be both black and American in a nation that constantly inundates them with negative images, many black Americans accept and act out what others describe of them. As Frederick Douglass wrote, "If from the cradle through life the outside world brands a class as unfit for this work or that work, the character of the class will come to resemble and conform to the character described."[2] More recently, Ellis Cose wrote, "One reason we can be so deadly to each other is that our environment encourages us to be that way. I am not speaking only of the neighborhoods in which we live, where, too often, violence is a way of life, but of the broader cultural environment as well, where racial stereotypes (particularly the one of the brutal black buck) refuse to die."[3] If black Americans are to survive the twenty-first century, the black church must help develop a culture where each black American feels like a *somebody*, especially in wider culture where they often feel like a *nobody*. The black church must teach and preach the Bible from an Afrocentric perspective to show the beauty of blackness in the scriptures. The black church must change the white images of Jesus Christ and other biblical characters wherever they are in the black church and replace them with images that reflect their racial identity. The black church must point out all the inventions that came from the mind of black people, and encourage self-support with black businesses that do exist.

The survival and liberation of black people depends largely on what they think of themselves and on their willingness to relate with each other to create a different world than the one created for them. Until the oppressed purge themselves of the consciousness of their oppressors, their behavior will continue to work at cross-purposes with their liberation. Paulo Freire analyzed the way the oppressor prescribes the behavior of the oppressed, determining that the oppressed

> are fearful of freedom. Freedom would require them to eject this image
> [that the oppressor creates of them] and replace it with autonomy and
> responsibility. Freedom is acquired by conquest, not by gift. It must be
> pursued constantly and responsibly. Freedom is not an ideal located out
> side of man; nor is it an ideal which becomes myth. It is rather the
> indispensable condition for the quest for human completion. . . . Although
> the situation of oppression is a dehumanized and dehumanizing totality
> affecting both the oppressors and those whom they oppress, it is the latter
> who must, from their stifled humanity, wage for both the struggle for a
> fuller humanity; the oppressor, who is himself dehumanized because he
> dehumanizes others, is unable to lead this struggle.[4]

The struggle for the oppressed to have a fuller humanity falls on the
shoulders of the oppressed. The initiation for transformation will not come
from the oppressors; it must come from those who are oppressed. The black
church must take the initiative and necessary risk to bring about a new situation. It must critically find ways in dealing with the consciousness of black
America in the pursuit of creating a new situation. Carroll A. Watkins Ali
calls for the black church to meet not only the spiritual needs but also the
psychological needs of a racially oppressed people.

> What the Black church needs to recognize is that many of its people suffer
> tremendous psychological burdens. Although there are many possibilities
> as to why, there are two major reasons why the Black church needs to
> address the psychological aspects of persons along with the spiritual. First,
> psychological burdens may be caused by deep spiritual conflicts, often cre
> ated by theology that is oppressive. Secondly, many suffer from
> psychological problems as a result of the physical and psychological oppres
> sion that we as a people have experienced for as long as we have been in
> this country. If African Americans are going to survive and be liberated, we
> must intentionally provide pastoral care that allows for counseling that
> addresses the psychological along with the spiritual.[5]

More than February

Overcoming black oppression and its psychological manifestations must be a
top priority for the black church in the twenty-first century. One month in

February to recognize black achievement and promote worth and self-love in a people is not enough. Because of centuries of oppression and distortions concerning black people, the black church must consistently address and demonstrate black people's inherent worth by constantly lifting up their history and struggling against unjust social structures that create psychological problems for them. The black church must do this without fear of offending the power structure. When the black church addresses and counsels the psychological as well as the spiritual needs of black people, then it is a relevant church. Martin Luther King Jr. said, "Any religion that professes to be concerned with the souls of men and yet is not concerned with the economic and social conditions that strangle them and the social conditions that cripple them is the kind the Marxist describes as 'an opiate of the people.'"[6] To achieve what he has described will take more than the shortest month of the year. This transformation will take years because the damage done to the psyche of black people happens over a period of centuries. The black church must consistently treat the psychological effects of oppression.

Shackled Minds

The black church must deal with all aspects of correcting oppression, and the psychological transformation of the oppressed is the most challenging. Centuries of wounding and shaping the consciousness of the oppressed by the oppressor require time to heal and reshape, but the black church must work to do it consistently. The black church should never expect the oppressors to give it a blueprint on how to free the minds of the oppressed when oppressors depend largely on the economic support of the oppressed to remain privileged. Oppressed groups win liberation not by the willing generosity of their oppressors but by their own demands and struggles.

Amos Wilson observed how the consciousness of the oppressed serves the interest of the oppressor:

> Oppressors produce a consciousness in the oppressed not only by manipulating their ecological and sociological lifestyles and possibilities but also by naming the world in which both they and the oppressed exist. To name, to label, is to bring into consciousness and therefore to transform consciousness. In empowering themselves to name the world and to reinforce their naming of it, oppressors empower themselves to construct the social reality and the consciousness of the oppressed in ways compatible with their interests. The social reality and consciousness of the oppressed as forged by

their oppressors motivate them to functionally perpetuate their own oppression.[7]

To change this situation, the black church must encourage a percentage of its constituency to be trained in mentoring and counseling along with its trained pastoral counselors. If more at-risk youth could receive emotional and spiritual support from role models they respect, they will learn to love themselves and take pride in making productive choices. Trinity United Church of Christ in Chicago focuses its whole ministry on helping blacks to love and support themselves. Their motto is "Unashamedly Black and Unapologetically Christian." This church has had great success in raising awareness of the roles of black people in biblical history.

Without the transformation of the mind, the condition of the oppressed will grow worse. We cannot afford to continue to allow this to happen to an already wounded and dying people.

Cornel West wrote, "The most basic issue now facing black America [is] the nihilistic threat . . . of psychological depression, personal worthlessness, and social despair."[8] This self-destructive behavior and the resignation of meaning, love, and hope are so pervasive among black America that it is frightening to imagine our future in the next fifty years. Psychological transformation is key in helping black Americans. The Scriptures teach us in Romans 12:2 not to conform to the world and its systems of oppression. Instead, it tells us to "be transformed by the renewing of your minds, so that you may discern what is the will of God" (RSV). Unless the minds of black Americans are transformed, or set free from a consciousness that causes them to carry out the interest of the oppressor, no systematic change will be possible for them. They will operate in such a way that their liberation and well-being can never be achieved. Carter G. Woodson stated, "The problem of holding the Negro down therefore is easily solved. When you control a man's thinking you do not have to worry about his actions. You do not have to tell him to stand here or go yonder. He will find his 'proper place' and will stay in it. You do not need to send him to the back door; he will cut one for his own special benefit. His education makes it necessary."[9] I would add that his religion makes it necessary, his worldview makes it necessary, his socialization makes it necessary, and his consciousness makes it necessary. The thinking of a people must change if their conditions are to change.

No Pie-in-the-Sky Solution

The black church must do more than treat oppression by promising a rescue intervention from on high, by preaching and singing, "You can have this world but just give me Jesus." We all need Jesus to help us struggle against institutional structures of oppression. However, Jesus taught and demonstrated God's will on earth as it is in heaven. We get nowhere by resigning this world to oppressors and then begging God to meet our needs. In the twenty-first century, we face the mental illness of a people that causes them to practice genocide on themselves. The "pie-in-the-sky" fantasy is not working. Frederick Douglass, Harriet Tubman, Martin Luther King Jr., and other freedom fighters realized that no other agent would come to do for them what they could do for themselves. Fantasies only create a counterrevolutionary attitude in the oppressed so that they look for salvation outside themselves. Black people need a consciousness that counters their oppression, not one that cooperates with it. Too often, the black church fails to assist black people in developing the kind of consciousness they need to struggle against their oppression. Without a transformed consciousness, black people "blithely nurture and protect a system which exploits and blinds them to its intrinsically evil purpose, and its ultimate deadly intent. Thus, compensatory fantasy under oppression often comes to characterize, as a necessary adjunct to the oppressive regime, the 'normal' consciousness of the oppressed."[10] The black church must work aggressively to heal and transform the minds of the oppressed.

Thinking for Themselves

Black Americans must think for themselves and not depend on someone else's thoughts. Doing our own thinking is the first step toward mental liberation. Freeing the mind is central for the transformation of a people. Chinweizu understood this when he said,

> The central objective in decolonizing the African mind is to overthrow the authority which alien traditions exercise over the African. This demands the dismantling of white supremacists beliefs, and the structures which uphold them. . . . Economic and political control can never be complete or effective without mental control. To control a people's culture is to control their tools of self-definition in relationship with others.[11]

Until there is a reconstruction of values that serve to maintain oppression, oppressed people will continue to work at cross-purposes with their own liberation.

Carter G. Woodson insists that to have a psychological conversion, we must break from the miseducation and misreligion we were taught. "In chameleon-like fashion, the Negro has taken up almost everything religious which has come along instead of thinking for himself," wrote Woodson. "It is clear, then, that if the Negro got their conception of religion from slaveholders, libertines, and murderers, there may be something wrong about it, and it would not hurt to investigate it."[12] The black church must reassess what and why it believes. To free the black community psychologically, economically, socially, and politically, the black church must interpret and direct the destiny of the community. Black people rely too much on others for direction and interpretation.

Part of the problem with the plight of black people is their failure to do their own thinking, and many do not think because they do not read. When people do not read, others easily mislead or dupe them. Naim Akbar stated, "The nature of our problem is quite serious and represents a deeply embedded psychological disturbance. We need something more than an aspirin to remove the symptoms. We need massive corrective surgery on the brain!"[13]

More black churches need to promote literacy programs within the church. Some churches (e.g., the African Methodist Episcopal church and the Christian Methodist Episcopal church) are taking literacy training in their churches seriously. Perhaps churches could create book clubs in which youth and adults are encouraged to read selected texts that would help them develop comprehension skills and educate them on topics relevant to their lives. The more churches get involved in literacy training, the more the black community can transform itself economically, socially, politically, and emotionally. Black churches must aggressively convey the benefits of reading and help demonstrate that reading opens the mind both to the world and to new, empowering ideas. An excellent example of inspirational reading is the classic autobiography of Frederick Douglass. He risked his life to learn to read and later became a great orator and leader because he understood the connection between literacy and liberation.

Improved literacy would assist black people in getting rid of the false consciousness they developed due to oppression and marginalization. To change the way blacks think of themselves and the way they treat each other, their minds must undergo conversion.

Brain Development and Resulting Behavior

We must understand that from the time our brains are capable of cognition, we began to form ideas, worldviews, and presuppositions that determine our presumed destiny. What we allow to go into the brain shapes our behavior and psychological environment and sets in motion our perception of reality. This is why it is essential to protect the minds of children, who are impressionable and easily influenced. Books, movies, television, and the radio are mediums of communication that conspire to shape psychological and cultural perceptions. If images of black people in general and black men in particular are constantly negative and self-debasing, studies show that often these people act out the perceptions others attribute to them. Billy Hawkins points out in his article "The White Supremacy Continuum of Images for Black Men" that the social construction of certain images within mass media fosters attitudes and behaviors that prohibit healthy social and race relations.[14] Frederick Douglass also discovered this in the nineteenth century when he said, "If from the cradle through life the outside world brands a class as unfit for this or that work, the character of the class will come to resemble and conform to the character described. To find valuable qualities in our fellows, such qualities must be presumed and expected."[15] For example, if people perceive black men as a menace to society, thuggish characters, brutes, oversexed school dropouts, drug dealers, criminals, etc., and black men live out these perceptions attributed to them, a falsification of black male consciousness is created, leading black males toward a life of mayhem and self-destruction. Behavior often rises to the level of the expectation.

Negative Psychodynamic Effects

Because black people do not control the media and communication outlets that portray them to the world, they are often cast in a negative light. The negative images of black people keep them in a state of frustration and self-contempt. This is not to convey that all black people behave in the ways they are portrayed. However, when they are cast as the poster people for crime, drugs, dependency, and all that is low and base in our society, other people naturally see them in this way. According to Amos Wilson, media images are "designed to inculcate within us a sense of inferiority and designed to keep us from facing reality and confronting the truth, to divert us from the pitifulness of our situation; to not let us recognize as a people that we are in a precarious situation, and that our very biological survival is in question."[16]

We must face the fact that the system we live under uses psycho-controls to keep oppressed people from developing the kind of consciousness that helps them solve their own problems. "Indeed," wrote Paulo Freire, "the interests of the oppressors lie in changing the consciousness of the oppressed, not the situation which oppresses them. . . . For the more the oppressed can be led to adapt to that situation, the more easily they can be dominated."[17] Oppression cannot be sustained without the manipulation of the consciousness to create a sense of powerlessness, and when this happens, the oppressed become apathetic. People give up and resign from life. As Amos Wilson wrote, "The fear of trusting and uniting with each other, the fear of coming together and solving our problems together, the belief that it is just not in us to unite and solve our own problems and overcome the dominance of European imperialism itself becomes a part of the problem and helps to maintain the system."[18]

The falsification of the consciousness of a people can lead them to hate themselves. He who hates himself "hates other people who remind him of himself. And therefore, when he looks out at his sisters and brothers he also looks at himself; and if he questions the adequacy and competence of himself; he questions the adequacy and competence of his sisters and brothers."[19] An alien consciousness is terribly effective at dominating the thoughts and actions of a people. It is all in the mind. Oppressive structures have shaped the minds of the oppressed to the point that they don't believe any kind of salvation lies within themselves. They think social, economic, and political liberation lies outside themselves. Thus, the oppressed wait for another agent to do for them what they can do for themselves.

Mind Problem

The black church must understand how psychological oppression affects the minds of the oppressed. Therefore, it is clear that black people don't have a money problem; they have a *mind problem*. They don't have an intelligence problem; they have a *mind problem*. They don't have a beauty problem; they have a *mind problem*. They don't have an opportunity problem; they have a *mind problem*. Until their consciousness changes, unless they undergo a psychological conversion, the frightening conditions in black America and the world will remain the same. Because black people have not broken the chains of psychological slavery, they fail to unite for their social and economic uplifting. Their minds are held captive and are desperate for liberation from the ideological rational that guides their perceptions, expectations, and actions. Too often, the consciousness of black people guides them to carry out the program of their oppressors. Until there is a purging of the ideas, beliefs, values, and ethics that are at the base of their cognitive awareness, black people will not overcome their oppression. In the words of Martin Luther King Jr.,

> As long as the mind is enslaved the body can never be free. Psychological freedom, a firm sense of self-esteem, is the most powerful weapon against the long night of physical slavery. No Lincolnian emancipation proclamation or Kennedyan or Johnsonian civil rights bill can totally bring this kind of freedom. The Negro will only be truly free when he reaches down to the inner depths of his own being and signs with the pen and ink of assertive selfhood his own emancipation proclamation.[20]

Some have made efforts to transform the conditions of black people, but their minds have gone untreated. The minds of black people must be treated first, and once the mind is treated and healed, then we can enjoy a new consciousness that will transform us from an old self to a new self. A new self creates the new conditions of which the once dependent self can now live independent and free. Liberation is the outcome of a new mind and new self.

The Remaining Key to Liberation

It is my belief that the remaining key to unlock black people's total liberation is mind transformation. It is imperative to help black people change the way they think and see reality. If the thinking is not changed, the actions will not change. The end results will always be the same: blacks undermining themselves while other groups use them to their advantage. A different result requires different thinking and different strategies. James Allen sheds light on the importance of developing the mind:

> Just as the gardener cultivates his plot, keeping it free from weeds, and growing the flowers and fruits which he requires, so may a [people] tend the garden of [their] mind, weeding out all the wrong, useless, and impure thoughts, and cultivating toward perfection the flowers and fruits of right, useful, and pure thoughts. By pursuing this process, a [people] sooner or later discover that [they] are the master-gardener of [their] soul, the director of [their] life. . . . When [they] realize that [they] are a creative power, and that [they] may command the hidden soil and seeds of [their] being

out of which circumstances grow, [they] then become the rightful master of [themselves]. . . .[21]

The black church must put its energy and resources into transforming the minds of the people, and we cannot do this if the black church is unwilling to make the necessary theological reconstruction that would free the oppressed from the stronghold of their psychological enslavement. The black church still conveys that, in order to have their needs met, the people must merely praise God. So the people praise God and give their resources, but their suffering social and economic situation remains the same. Benjamin Mays calls these compensatory beliefs, claiming that they keep the oppressed from developing a revolutionary spirit that will help them put an end to the ills they suffer. Many years ago, he observed,

> The Negro's social philosophy and his ideas of God go hand and hand. . . . Certain theological ideas enable Negroes to endure hardship, suffer pain, and withstand maladjustment, but . . . do not necessarily motivate them to strive to eliminate the source of the ills they suffer.
>
> Since this world is considered a place of temporary abode, many of the Negro masses have inclined to do little or nothing to improve their status here; they have been encouraged to rely on a just God to make amends in heaven for all the wrongs they have suffered on earth. . . . Believing this about God, the Negro . . . has stood back and suffered much without bitterness, without striking back, and without trying aggressively to realize to the full his needs in the world.[22]

The black church must change its way of thinking, teaching, and communicating to oppressed people. Holding the line of the status quo will not bring about the liberation of a people. Liberation must start in the minds of the oppressed if their actions are to counter their oppression. One way to do this is prescribed by Lerone Bennett Jr.:

> The overriding need for the moment is for us to think with our own mind. We cannot see now because our eyes are clouded by the concepts of white supremacy. We cannot think now because we have no intellectual instruments save those which were designed expressly to keep us from seeing. It is necessary for us to develop a new frame of reference, which transcends the limits of white concepts. White concepts have succeeded in making black people feel inferior. White concepts have created the conditions that make it easy to dominate a people. The initial step towards liberation is to

abandon the partial frame of reference of our oppressor and to create new concepts which release our reality.[23]

Correct Education

We constantly convey that education is the key to rescuing people from an undesirable predicament, and I agree. However, we must emphasize the kind of education. In many ways, black people are victims of miseducation. With numerous educated blacks, why is there still strife, anger, bitterness, and self-sabotage among us? Why have educated blacks not come together to pool their intelligence and strategize in a way that helps bring the race out of its death trap? Has our education made us better or pushed us further apart? Our education in rugged individualism has only hindered us. Any people who have received an education that teaches them to act alone instead of acting as a group in an oppressive society is miseducated. Blacks have been educated not to practice group dynamics, and this is the reason the best minds and monetary resources have not worked for blacks as a whole. Black people are educated in separation and division.

We must emphasize blacks receiving correct education. Amos Wilson insisted,

> We are now at the crossroads. We are in a pathetic situation as far as the world is concerned. We are in a situation that is exceeding dangerous, where we are questioning whether Afrikan peoples survive the next century. And consequently it's going to take a different kind of thinking style, a different system of values, and a different approach to human relations to get us out of this quandary that we are in today; the quandary the European has put us in. And it's going to require a different kind of education than what is available today.[24]

Unless oppressed people receive an education that gives them a new consciousness to transform their social situation, their lot in this world will not improve. Richard Shaull writes, "Education either functions as an instrument that is used to facilitate the integration of the younger generation into the logic of the present system and bring about conformity to it, or it becomes the practice of freedom, the means by which men and women deal critically and creatively with reality and discover how to participate in the transformation of their world."[25] The kind of education people receive indicates whether or not they will participate in the transformation of society.

Elijah Muhammad stated, "We need education, but an education which removes us from the shackles of slavery and servitude. Get an education, but not an education which leaves us in an inferior position and without a future. Get an education, but not an education that leaves us looking to the slavemaster for a job."[26]

The church needs to emphasize an education that helps people know themselves so they won't continue to be what others say they are. For a long time, oppressed people have operated the way they have been taught, and since we are creatures of habit, it is difficult to get us to work on developing a new consciousness. Even so, the black church must encourage it. Education about self will turn people from self-sabotage and self-annihilation to self-love and self-reliance. Self-destruction happens when people feel they are of no significance and have not contributed to the development and civilization of the world. Why live when you believe you have no self-worth? The black church must create an environment of self-worth among oppressed people by by encouraging education, developing literacy training, teaching and preaching from a Afrocentric perspective, pointing out blacks' great contributions and inventions, providing counseling and mentors, encouraging and supporting black businesses in the community, and creating an environment for the youth to learn and develop. This is the only way they will develop a mentality to participate in their own transformation. This is the only way they will develop a mentality to participate in their own transformation.

Unless the black church can help to rid the black community of destructive behavior and engage the community in liberating actions that accent economic, social, and political liberation, its contingency will continue to abandon the black church as irrelevant. There is not much time remaining. We must act now or perish. The choice is ours. We must straighten up our backs and throw off the manacles of psychological slavery and reclaim faith in God and in ourselves. I remind the black church of what Nehemiah said to his people centuries ago: "You see the trouble we are in" (Neh 2:17)? If we see, we must act now! Time is running out.

Paul Robeson reminds us,

> We must realize that our future lies chiefly in our own hands. We know that neither institution nor friends can make a race stand unless it has strength in its own foundation; that races like individuals must stand or fall by their own merit; that to fully succeed they must practice the virtues of self-reliance, self respect, industry, perseverance, and economy.[27]

When the black church creates a process for the liberation of the oppressed by helping the oppressed eject the consciousness of their oppressors that causes contradiction, division, and trauma to the psyche of oppressed people, then it becomes relevant for the twenty-first century. However, if the black church chooses to remain in its present business-as-usual state, advancing survival models of existence rather than liberation models for a new humanity, its irrelevance will become more and more acute. The choice is ours today. As James Cone asked,

> Are we going to continue to preach the same old sermons, pray the same old prayers, and sing the same old songs as if that alone would be enough for the establishment of freedom in the twenty-first century? Are we going to continue with the same old church meetings and conferences—electing officers and bishops, holding revivals and hearing charismatic speakers, buying old white churches and constructing new ones, appointing and calling pastors on the basis of a superficial emotional appeal, shouting and testifying for the saints, while the world around us continues toward destruction?[28]

It is my hope that the black church makes a paradigm shift in its thinking and starts working anew on liberating the suffering masses of people at home and abroad. We must awaken to the realization that we have been given the Spirit of Christ to help solve the problems of the world. Christianity is not merely soul salvation; it is also body, mind, and community salvation. For the church to continue business as usual means God's people will forever be held in the psychological bondage of their oppression. Our children and grandchildren will continue to suffer because we were afraid to develop the mind of Jesus Christ not only in us but also in our children. The mind of Christ said no to oppression, no to exploitation, no to powerlessness, no to inferiority, and no to the things that make life a nightmare and an unending holocaust. Until we develop the mind of Christ in us, the future of black Americans will be a repeat of the past and present condition. However, I do put hope in these words: "The frontiers are never closed; the limits of progress are never reached. The future will be what we ourselves make it. . . . The most challenging opportunity of all history lies before us."[29]

Notes

1. W. E. B. Du Bois, *The Souls of Black Folk* (New York: Penguin, 1969) 45–46.

2. Frederick Douglass, *Life and Times of Frederick Douglass* (New York: Macmillan Publishing Company, 1962) 474.

3. Ellis Cose, *The Envy of the World* (New York: Washington Square Press, 2002) 59.

4. Paulo Freire, *Pedagogy of the Oppressed* (New York: Continuum, 1999) 28–29.

5. Carroll A. Watkins Ali, *Survival and Liberation: Pastoral Theology in African American Context* (St. Louis: Chalice Press, 1999) 156.

6. Martin Luther King Jr., *Strength to Love* (Philadelphia: Fortress Press, 1963) 101.

7. Amos N. Wilson, *The Falsification of Afrikan Consciousness* (New York: Afrikan World InfoSystems, 1993) 117–18.

8. Cornel West, *Race Matters* (New York: Vintage Books, 1994) 19.

9. Carter G. Woodson, *The Miseducation of the Negro* (Washington DC: Associated Publishers, Inc., 1933, 1969) xxxiii.

10. Wilson, *The Falsification of Afrikan Consciousness*, 127–28.

11. Cited in Naim Akbar, *Know Thy Self* (Tallahassee: Mind Productions & Associates, 1998) ii.

12. Woodson, *The Miseducation of the Negro*, 58, 73.

13. Naim Akbar, *Breaking the Chains of Psychological Slavery* (Tallahassee: Mind Productions & Associates, 1996) 51–52.

14. Billy Hawkins, "The White Supremacy Continuum of Images for Black Men," *Journal of African American Studies* 3/3 (December 1998).

15. Douglass, *The Life and Times of Frederick Douglass,* 425.

16. Wilson, *The Falsification of Afrikan Consciousness*, 70–71.

17. Paulo Freire, *Pedagogy of the Oppressed* (New York: Continuum Publishing Company, 1993) 55.

18. Wilson, *The Falsification of Afrikan Consciousness*, 75.

19. Ibid., 74.

20. Martin Luther King Jr., "Where Do We Go from Here," in *A Testament of Hope*, ed. James Melvin Washington (San Francisco: Harper & Row Publishers, 1986) 582.

21. Cited in *Light From Many Lamps*, ed. Lillian Eichler Watson (New York: Simon & Schuster, 1951) 170–71.

22. Benjamin E. Mays, *The Negro's God* (New York: Atheneum, 1969) 155.

23. Lerone Bennett Jr., *The Challenge of Blackness* (Chicago: Johnson Publishing Company, 1972) 36.

24. Amos N. Wilson, *Awakening the Natural Genius of Black Children* (New York: Afrikan World Infosystems, 1991) 1.

25. Cited from Shaull's foreword to Paulo Freire, *Pedagogy of the Oppressed*, 16.

26. Cited in Naim Akbar, *Know Thy Self* (Tallahassee: Mind Productions & Associates, 1998) 58.

27. *Famous Black Quotations*, selected and compiled by Janet Cheatham Bell, (Chicago IL: Sabayt Publications, 1986) 56.

28. Cone, *For My People*, 197.

29. Lillian E. Watson, ed., *Light from Many Lamps* (New York: Simon & Schuster, 1951) 280–81.

Discussion Questions

1. What "negative and distorted images" might black people believe about themselves? What do whites believe about black people? How do these images affect the way black people treat each other and the way society treats them?

_____

_____

_____

_____

2. The author quotes Cornel West, who wrote, "The most basic issue now facing black America [is] the nihilistic threat . . . of psychological depression, personal worthlessness, and social despair." In what practical ways can churches heighten the self-confidence of troubled people? How might feeling like "a *somebody*" help a black individual make better choices?

_____

_____

_____

_____

3. In what ways do many black Americans depend on the thoughts of other people rather than on their own perspectives? What typically determines the social and economic position of blacks? How can blacks change this?

_____

_____

_____

_____

4. The author writes, "The black church must change its way of thinking, teaching, and communicating to oppressed people." How does the black church currently do these things? In what practical ways could it change direction?

_____

_____

_____

_____

5. How has our culture failed in educating black Americans (i.e., in areas of literacy, sex education, parenting techniques, marital commitment, money management, etc.)? What is the church's role in the education of black people? How would greater education help break the current destructive cycle among many black youth?

_____

_____

_____

_____

Chapter 4

THE WHITE CHURCH'S PARTICIPATORY ROLE

"[We] have become irrelevant to the faith communities that we claim to represent. . . . Theology has indeed become academic."
　　　　　—Roberto Goizueta, President of the Catholic Theological Seminary of America, 2004–2005

Church Division

When Christ stated in Matthew 12:25 that "Every Kingdom divided against itself is brought to desolation; and every city or house divided against itself shall not stand," he never imaged nor intended that the church he established would be an example of this division. The church has been divided for centuries across racial lines, and for this reason it has not been able to carry out its purpose and mission in the world. When the modern-day church could have been a mighty force in the world struggling together with both arms against wrong, evil, and injustice, it decided to use one arm and bind the other. The bound arm is the people of African descent who were enslaved and oppressed by the legitimization justification of the white church. Because the church allowed color prejudice to drive a wedge between the members of the body of Christ, the black church was forced into being. Because of racism, white and black churches have been divided over the centuries. Bad theology and pseudo-science have taught the inferiority of black people, causing a rift in the relationship between the two groups. Therefore, genuine brotherhood and sisterhood are hindered. H. Richard Niebuhr made this observation years ago:

> Rationalization has been used to defend discrimination rather than to obscure it. The dogma which divides the racial churches is anthropological, not theological, in content. Whether the dogma of white superiority and Negro inferiority has been openly avowed or unconsciously accepted, the white churches have nevertheless taken it for granted and have come to regard it as not incompatible with the remainder of their beliefs. At times, indeed, they have incorporated it in their popular theology and sought to provide a biblical basis for it, usually by means of a mythological interpretation of the curse of Ham and a corresponding mythological anthropology.[1]

The spirit of white supremacy invaded the church, and instead of the white church being an ally and support for suffering black brothers and sisters in Christ, the church either sided with current perceptions of blacks, or remained silent as they watched the inhumanity of God's people. Much of the oppression and injustice inflicted upon blacks could have been avoided if not eliminated had the white church banished white supremacy from its ranks and dictated how to receive and treat other members of God's family. Had more leaders and authentic Christians of the white church preached and practiced the commonwealth of God and the beloved community, prejudice and discrimination would not have festered for decades in American life. Like the black church, the white church often fulfills a mission contrary to the purpose for which it was established. Amos Jones Jr. wrote, "The history of the white church in this country has been bogged down in bigotry, hindered by hypocrisy, restrained by racism, hampered by half-heartedness, entangled in the webbing of a twisted theology, and inhibited by so many other factors that the church has been prevented from running a creditable Christian race."[2] In a real sense, the white church has contradicted the gospel and the apostolic creed of oneness in Christ.

I do not want to devalue the contributions of whites who have struggled, sacrificed, and died for the cause of righteousness and justice in our land. Many have worked to make our land freer and more humane. I believe "that there are many good people in the world but there are very few who are good enough to disturb the devil."[3] Though a few whites have struggled against inhumanity, the great majority refuses to disturb what the devil is doing.

While blacks were "despised, insulted, ignored, whipped, cudgeled, hunted down by bloodhounds, seized by mobs and slashed and burned and hanged and blown to pieces," the white church remained silent.[4] Worse, white ministers and theologians by and large were more interested in law and order, which was really ordered injustice, than they were in justice for black people. Their interpretation of the gospel message was quiet on the subject of racial oppression. The gospel was preached in such a way that it became an integral part of a society that denied blacks the right to freedom and equality. The experiences of black Americans went unacknowledged, and their plight was not reflected upon during theological discourse. America dismissed black suffering and oppression into invisibility. Refusing to see the suffering and oppression of a people caused that people's social reality to worsen. I have given adequate attention to the black church and its leaders, and it is my hope to raise the consciousness of the white church so it can join Christ in the struggle against oppression, evil, and injustice.

Racial Division

The truth often cuts, but it is necessary for healing. Too often, the white church has allowed racial division without aggressively trying to overcome the separation of Christians based upon race. The most segregated time in America is still the eleven o'clock worship hour on Sundays. Christians have not made much progress along racial lines. Mixed congregations exist, but white pastors lead most of them. Rarely do we see white congregations headed by black pastors. Racial separation of Christians is the moral failure of Western Christianity. Not only has racial separation weakened the church's effective witness in the world, but has also turned people away from the church because it is no less than a replica of other social institutions. The love of Christ spoken of in the white church stays in the white church. The practice of what is spoken hardly ever goes beyond the narrow confines of where it is spoken. The orthodoxy of love, justice, and brotherhood is rarely an orthopraxy in the inner cities and urban areas where people are victims of structural, social, and economic injustice. "It is a sad fact that the white church's involvement in slavery and racism in America simply cannot be overstated," wrote James Cone. "It not only failed to preach the kerygmatic Word but maliciously contributed to the doctrine of white supremacy. Even today all of the Church's institutions—including its colleges and universities—reveal its white racist character."[5] Some, like Fred D. Wentzel, have tried to help white Christians understand the nonsense of racism within the body of Christ. Six decades ago, Wentzel stated the predicament of white Christians, and it still resonates today:

> This is our predicament: when we say "our nation" we seem to include every citizen, but actually we mean "the white man's nation"; when we pray "Our Father" we seem to include all the members of God's family, but actually we mean "The white man's Father." We are therefore never saying what we mean, in politics or in religion. We are incapable of giving ourselves wholly, without reservations, to democracy or to Christianity.[6]

The white church must understand what the malignancy of racism has done and still does to the body of Christ. The spirit of racism must be destroyed if God's people are to come together and build the kingdom of God. The responsibility of destroying racism is largely on the shoulders of whites who created it and maintain it. Due to the power whites have gained through slavery, segregation, and exploitation of black people, whites have a greater responsibility to correct the wrong. Blacks must play their part in their own transformation by doing those things that would help bring them out of their oppression, but we must keep in mind that black oppression is a direct result of white power. Unless whites get the mountain lion of racism out of the way, Christianity's goals and purposes can never be realized. After all, as Wentzel wrote,

> If the gospel of reconciliation cannot even bring its own devotees of various colors together . . . , who will believe that it has power to heal the racial divisions in industry, social life and international relations? The church must continue to be weak and self-defeating in its efforts to create in its own attitude and practice an all-inclusive fellowship. It is now a very sick man telling everybody how to be well.[7]

Understanding Racism

There is much talk about blacks being racists like whites and that both groups must stop practicing racism. It is true that groups must get rid of the "isms" that divide them. However, blacks do not practice racism, for racism relates to power dynamics that blacks do not possess. Blacks can certainly be prejudiced like whites, but they cannot be racists because blacks do not own and control institutions under which whites must live. Joseph Barndt stated that racism is developed when one racial group becomes so powerful and dominant that it is able to control another group and to enforce the controlling group's biases. . . . Racism (prejudice plus power) develops when personal opinion and individual bigotry are codified and enforced as societal behavior. Racism structures a society so that the prejudices of one racial group are taught, perpetuated and enforced to the benefit of the dominant group.[8]

It is true that groups without power may have prejudiced views of other groups who hold power, but these prejudiced views do not cause suffering like the views of groups who hold power. For example, blacks do not own and control institutions under which whites have to live, but whites do own and control institutions under which black have to live. Institutional racism has and still does affect black people today. Andrew Hacker wrote, "The significance of racism lies in the way it consigns certain human beings to the margin of society, if not to painful lives and early deaths. In the United States, racism takes its highest toll on blacks. No white person can claim to have suffered in such ways because of ideas that may be held about them by some black citizens."[9] Because of slavery and trans-generational oppression, whites have built a power structure in which blacks suffer and are destroyed. For centuries, blacks have struggled against this kind of unjust social and economic structure. As William R. Jones stated, "The alleged superior group has the most of whatever society defines as the best, and the least of the worst. In stark contrast, the alleged inferior group will have the least of the best and the most of the worst."[10]

The white church must understand the power dynamics of racism and oppression and join forces with blacks who struggle against this kind of arrangement. Refusing to help struggling blacks who are constant victims of this unjust arrangement constitutes agreement with it. Acknowledging that this arrangement is unfair and not aggressively working to correct constitutes hypocrisy. Andrew Hacker made an important observation:

> White people who disavow responsibility deny an everyday reality: that to be black is to be consigned to the margins of American life. It is because of this that no white American, including those who insist that opportunities exist for persons of every race, would change places with even the most successful black American. All white Americans realize that their skin comprises an inestimable asset. It opens doors and facilitates freedom of movement. It serves as a shield from insult and harassment. Indeed, having been born white can be taken as a sign: your preferment is both ordained and deserved. Its value persists not because a white appearance automati-

cally brings success and status, since there are no such guarantees. What it does ensure is that you will not be regarded as black, a security that is worth so much that no one who has it has ever given it away.[11]

Why Some Blacks Reject Christianity

To understand why some blacks feel that Christianity is a white man's religion is to understand how Christianity was practiced toward them over the years. E. Franklin Frazier stated it this way:

> Not only did Christianity fail to offer the Negro hope of freedom in this world, but [also] the manner in which Christianity was communicated to him tended to degrade him. The Negro was taught that his enslavement was due to the fact that he had been cursed by God. His very color was a sign of the curse which he had received as a descendant of Ham [Gen 9:20-27]. Parts of the Bible were carefully selected to prove that God had intended that the Negro should be a servant of the white man and that he would always be a hewer of wood and a drawer of water.[12]

This kind of bad theology and interpretation goes against what Christ stood for in his ministry on earth. White Christianity sided with the system of oppression in keeping blacks disenfranchised. To preach about the love of God and then hate and mistreat blacks because of the color of their skin understandably repelled some blacks. The practice of a religion tells what people truly believe in their hearts. No wonder John said, "If any one says, 'I love God,' and hates his brother, he is a liar; for he who does not love his brother whom he has seen, cannot love God whom he has seen" (1 John 4:20, RSV). White Christianity created the "Hermeneutics of Suspicion" by their behavior and mistreatment of blacks, and therefore some blacks embraced other religions like Islam to promote their dignity and self-worth. White Christianity is infected with racism. William R. Jones stated, "Once it is concluded that Christianity is infected with 'Whitianity,' once it is granted that a racist doctrine of the tradition has been perpetuated, the tradition must be scrutinized in the most radical and comprehensive manner . . . and if it is found to be infected with the virus of racism and oppression, it must be cast aside."[13]

Whites may say that they do not practice prejudice and exclusivity in their churches. If this is true, why is Sunday still the most segregated day in America? Why is there still an imbalance of power between the two groups?

Why is the white church silent about the double standards and racial profiling in our land? Why are programs such as affirmative action attacked across the country when they have achieved what they set out to do—to give disenfranchised blacks a hand up? Notice what is stated here: a hand *up* not a hand out. Due to centuries of discrimination and exploitation, blacks were thrown behind socially, economically, and politically. Programs like affirmative action are at least one way to give a disinherited people a chance to catch up and bridge the gap created by racism and discrimination. To cry that affirmative action is preferential treatment is to miss the historical treatment of a people that put them at a disadvantage in the first place. Oppressed people can never have preferential treatment because of the power imbalance between the oppressed and their oppressors. Blacks suffer from a deficit of power while whites have an overwhelming surplus of power. Many white Christians oppose affirmative action. They do not understand what racism and oppression have done to black people. They feel that being part of the dominant group entitles to the dominant group's privileges and access, regardless of how this came into being.

The Cry of Reverse Discrimination

In an effort to correct the unjust situation of racism and oppression, many white Christians claim reverse discrimination. They accuse the minority group of preferential treatment. Andrew Hacker wrote,

> This helps to explain why white conservatives so vehemently oppose programs like affirmative action. They simply do not want to admit to themselves that the value imputed to being white has injured people who are black. Nor is this reaction surprising. Most people do not like feeling guilty. It can be an unpleasant, even painful, sensation. Hence the tendency to turn, often angrily, on those who stir us in this way. Rather than do something substantial to help people who have been treated unfairly, we find ourselves saying that they brought their afflictions on themselves.[14]

To blame victims for their oppression is like telling a rape victim it was her fault she was violated. The perpetrators view themselves as the victims and accuse the true victims of being at fault. Whites who cry discrimination feel that their jobs and their dreams are eroded at the expense of blacks getting a position over them. They do not understand that the system is designed to favor whites despite the qualifications of blacks. Therefore, when people try to correct this situation of discrimination and unfairness, some whites feel cheated. The truth of the matter is that the system was not designed on an equal playing field. Now that some whites feel the pinch of competition when it did not previously exist, they are embittered. The claim of reverse discrimination is a false one. Until whites understand and affirm that the system has been and still is unfair, tension between the two groups will remain.

The Schism Remains

The schism between black and white Christians continues with no sign of healing. The racism accepted in the white church remains as a sign of caste hostility. H. Richard Niebuhr observed,

> The racial schism instead of slowing any signs of healing . . . is steadily growing more acute. . . . The causes of the racial schism are not difficult to determine. Neither theology nor polity furnished the occasion for it. The sole source of this denominationalism is social; it demonstrates clearly the invasion of the church of Christ by the principles of caste. And this caste sense is, as always, primarily present in the economically and culturally superior group, and secondarily, by reaction, in the economically and culturally inferior society.
>
> Negroes have apparently taken the initiative in forming separate churches, but the responsibility lies with the former masters in the North and South. These made the independent church movement inevitable by the attitude which they adopted toward the colored Christians. Their unquestioned assumption of superior privileges, their unconscious wounding of the Negro self-respect, their complacent acceptance of the morality of the world as fitting for the church, have once more divided the body of Christ along the lines of social class. . . . Caste hostility leads to inevitable suspicions and misunderstanding even in the church.[15]

Fallacious assumptions of white supremacy and black inferiority must be eradicated if the white church is to be an instrument in the hand of God through Christ to transform society. Racism is the spirit of the antichrist, and the only way to get rid of it is through the power of the Holy Spirit. The white church needs healing from racism, but by denying that racism exists in the body of Christ and that the white church perpetuates it, it will never find healing. Paul Rogat Loeb stated, "As the Ethiopian proverb says, 'He who conceals his disease cannot be cured.' We need to understand our cultural diseases of callousness, shortsightedness, and denial, and learn what it will take to heal our society and heal our souls."[16] The process of healing can only take place when there is an acknowledgment that a disease exists and an adequate assessment is given to develop a vaccine.

National Advisory Commission on Civil Disorder

Although the white church has acknowledged in some ways the sin of racism, what white Christians may not know and understand is how deeply racism has affected black people. The government conducted a study called the Kerner Report of 1968 that acknowledged the disease of racism to help the nation chart a new course. The report stated,

> Our nation is moving toward two societies, one black, one white—separate and unequal. Racial prejudice, discrimination and segregation have shaped our history decisively; they now threaten the future of every American. Why did it happen? Certain fundamental matters are clear. Of these the most fundamental is the racial attitude and behavior of white Americans toward black Americans. . . . White racism is essentially responsible. . . . What white Americans have never fully understood, but what the Negro can never forget—is that white society is deeply implicated in the ghetto. White institutions created it, white institutions maintain it, and white society condones it.[17]

The white church must understand that racism is a virus that has lived within the body of Christ for a long time. White Christians have denied that it exists or have protected it while allowing it to mutate in such a way that it is more covert than overt today. A virus is much more dangerous in its covert form than when we can clearly see it. Racism must be exposed with all of its ugliness. Martin Luther King Jr. stated, "Like a boil that can never be cured as long as it is covered up, but must be opened with all its pus—flowing ugliness to the natural medicines of air and light, injustice must likewise be exposed, with all of the tension its exposing creates, to the light of human conscience and the air of national opinion before it can be cured."[18] The dirty laundry of racism can no longer stay within the clothes hamper of the Christian church. It must be brought out and washed in the cleansing agent of God's Word and the Holy Spirit. We must show the world that "There is neither Jew nor Greek, there is neither bond nor free, there is neither male nor female: for [we] are all one in Christ Jesus" (Gal 3:28). There must be a serious aggressive anti-racism movement within the white church that looks at racism, condemns it, and works to eliminate it. The good news is there are white churches such as World Harvest Church in Ohio, pastored by Rod Parsley, that are doing the very things just described. Multicultural churches are spreading across the nation, which is an attempt to move away from the past racist practices. Can more be done to bring the people of God together across racial lines? Yes, and the white church must continue in its efforts to bridge the gap between the races that have been separated by oppression, exploitation, lies, and hypocrisy.

The white church not only must preach against racism but must also be an agent of justice and liberation. It not only must be the Good Samaritan who aids the victim of violence and injustice, but it must also correct the situation that produces the violence and injustice. Paulo Freire stated, "To affirm that [people] are persons and as persons should be free, and yet do nothing tangible to make this affirmation a reality, is a farce."[19] The white church must do more than affirm the humanity of the oppressed. It must join them in the struggle to transform the structural injustice that produces violence against a people. As Fred Wentzel said, "The profound hunger of our time is not for brotherly words, but for brotherly deeds, not for the publishing of brave resolutions, but for the launching of brave experiments. . . . Let such action begin now, in the house of God!"[20]

Racism Is Not an Ancient Phenomenon

To eradicate a disease, it is necessary to trace its origin. What is the origin of racism, and why has it lasted so long within the body of Christ and the nation? Did color prejudice and racism beset early Christians? We can answer these questions by looking back in history. When one race of people disregards the history of another race of people, inevitably myths and stereotypes ensue. However, we can rid ourselves of myths and stereotypes through education and communication. If modern-day Christians studied ancient societies, they would know that racist attitudes based on skin complexion did not exist. Color was never the criterion for judging a people in the ancient world. It didn't exist as it does today. It is true that ancient authors of the biblical text were not color blind, but, as Cain Hope Felder wrote, "this consciousness of color and race was by no means a political or ideological basis for enslaving or otherwise oppressing other people."[21] The social structures were not designed to keep Africans or Ethiopians in their place because of skin complexion. Greeks were not amazed by the complexion of Africans.

Greeks and Romans showed no anti-black attitude toward Africans. Hostility based upon race was not a part of the cultural milieu.

Early Christian views of Ethiopians were in the same tradition as those of the Greco-Romans. The Greco-Roman world considered the Ethiopians highly intelligent people. Frank M. Snowden stated, "As late as the first century B.C. Ethiopians were presented to the Greco-Roman world by Diodorus as among civilization's 'pioneers,' and by writers of the early Roman Empire as renowned for their wisdom and for their fame in astrology."[22] An early Christian writer named Origen thought the Ethiopians were the symbol out of which the church was to grow:

> "Ethiopia shall stretch out her hands to God" and "from beyond the rivers of Ethiopia will I receive my dispersed ones." The hands of Ethiopia that is the people of the Gentiles in approaching God outstripped those to whom God's oracles had first been given. Israel by its failure had opened the way for the success of the Gentiles. It was thus, then, that the prophecy of the psalms was fulfilled and that the "black one" became beautiful, although the daughters of Jerusalem envied and reviled.[23]

In ancient days, Christianity was not the only religion that embraced Ethiopian blacks. The worship of Isis had an unprejudiced attitude toward Ethiopians. This Egyptian religion knew no color line or caste system to judge a people.

> Ethiopians were obviously welcomed as priests and cultists by Isis followers in Greece, Italy, and other centers of the cult, where their expert ritualistic knowledge and their authentic dances and music lent a note of genuineness to the ceremonies. A bond united black and white in the worship of a goddess who, in the words of R. E. Witt, "Came to win the unswerving love and loyalty of countless men and women of every rank . . . she did not allow room . . . for any prudery about sex or racial discrimination and segregation according to the color of one's skin."[24]

The nonsense of color prejudice in our day did not exist centuries ago. Charles B. Copher stated, "Early Christians failed to adopt the anti-black interpretations of the Jews, while the Muslim did; and . . . later, Gentile Christians, particularly in Europe, adopted the interpretations and applied them to black people whom they met in increasing numbers."[25]

Attitudes toward Africans or Ethiopian blacks were positive during the ancient and early days of Christianity because color played no role in marginalizing a people based upon race. The facts remain that Africans have con-tributed much to this world. Egypt, located in the heart of Africa, was the cradle of civilization, and many Western thinkers whom we hold in high esteem, from Socrates to Plato to Aristotle, received their education in Africa. Saint Augustine from North Africa laid down the theological princi-ples for the Western world. Many of the biblical characters to whom we refer in the church were Africans. Due to modern racism, though, the Western world has not recognized African people. From the time of the Enlightenment to the present day, Africans and their descendants have been made to feel that they are inferior and have contributed little to the world. Nothing is further from the truth. Black scholars are still refuting the claim of white supremacy. John Johnson, a black historical scholar, wrote these facts about black people:

> Since the beginning of earlier times from ancient Ethiopia and Egypt, Blacks (Negroes) played significant roles in developing nations and civiliza-tions. When the world was relatively uncivilized, the African Negroes were already working mathematics, using an alphabet, building pyramids, palaces, homes of brick, temples, yielding crops, raising livestock, melting metal that was molded into other objects, such as tools, weapons, and utensils. Blacks also excelled in the field of arts, literature, merchant, sci-ence, engineering, medicine, politics, religion, etc. This ancient civilization lasted for thousands of years, longer than any civilization known to man. It reached its peak and subsided long before Europe was born. There were others like Mali, Songhay, and Ghana who produced some of the finest universities and political structures in the world. Where at a time, untold numbers from abroad would visit Africa to seek knowledge. For centuries Blacks were in the highlight of all progress.[26]

Orientation in Miseducation

America would be a much greater nation if the contributions of blacks were made known and taught as part of America's school curriculum. However, modern racism made the judging of people's skin rather than their character the measuring instrument of acceptance. Both racial groups have had an ori-entation in miseducation. Many whites believe that their whiteness is a sign of divine favor that gives them the right to rule, define reality, and own and control the world's resources. Many blacks believe their blackness is a sign of divine disfavor that places them behind whites, where they must live under white authority. The miseducation of both groups has caused an unhealthy tension between them. It is my belief that white Christians, like black Christians, must learn to accept each other for their uniqueness, history, and contributions to world civilization. It is possible for white and black Christians to become the thermostats in setting the moral, ethical, and social temperature for the larger society and the world. What was done in the past does not have to be repeated in the present and future. We are not responsible for what has happened in the past, but we are responsible for what happens now and in the future. The white church must stop registering the temperature of society and start setting the temperature of society.

Spiritual (Not Racial) Warfare

The white church and its leaders must keep in mind that our warfare is spiritual rather than racial. We wrestle not against white, black, brown, and yellow flesh, "but against principalities, against powers, against the rulers of the darkness of this world, against spiritual wickedness in high places" (Eph 6:12). We are not saved based upon the color of our skin but upon the faith in our hearts. The blood Christ shed on Calvary for us was red, and it runs through the veins of every black, white, brown, and yellow person. To paraphrase Paul, "From one blood has God made all nations of people" (Acts 17:26). On an anthropological ground, then, we are the same. God our Creator did not give one race of people more attributes to prove its superiority over another, for "God is no respecter of persons" (Acts 10:34). God loves us all the same, and black people are just as significant in God's sight as the rest of God's children. The white church must rid itself of racism before it is too late. What spiritual and theological credibility can the white church have before the world in terms of human relations when it refuses to participate in the complete elimination of prejudice and discrimination within its own churches and conferences? Robert F. Kennedy stated, "The enemies of a solution to the racial dilemma are not the black man or the white man. The enemies are fear and indifference. They are hatred and, above all, letting monetary passion blind us to a clear and reasoned understanding of the realities of the land."[27]

This truth about the white church is not to judge them but to encourage repentance. Unless repentance takes place within the white church, there can be no reconciliation between the races. There can be no unity within the body of Christ. White Christians must unlearn their religious racism against nonwhite Christians. Habits are hard to break, especially since these habits have produced privileges over the centuries. If racism were not profitable for the white church, it would have been discarded years ago. Since it is profitable, the white church finds it difficult to stop practicing racism. However, Christ has never called us to give up something easy in order to follow him. Wealth, power, and privilege often get in the way of total commitment to Christ. When a rich ruler came to Christ and asked about eternal life, Jesus responded by saying, "Sell all that you own and distribute the money to the poor, and you will have treasure in heaven; then come, follow me." The rich man went away sad because he was very rich (Luke 18:22-23, RSV). Christ asks the same of the white church: give up things that are valuable, including racist behavior, and use the resources gained through a racist society to assist the poor, lift up the downtrodden, and release those held captive by economic, social, and political oppression. What Christ asks is not easy, but if the white church obeys, the reward is greater than the sacrifice. The white church has a choice—follow Christ or follow the cares of this world. If the white church decides to follow Christ, it can and must unlearn racism. The process won't be easy, but it is possible. Rick Warren wrote,

> We have a lot to unlearn. . . . There is no pill, prayer, or principle that will instantly undo the damage of many years. It requires the hard work of removal and replacement. The Bible calls it "taking off the old self" and "putting on the new self." . . . We are afraid to humbly face the truth about ourselves . . . the truth will set us free but it often makes us miserable first. The fear of what we might discover if we honestly faced our character defects keeps us living in the prison of denial. Only as God is allowed to shine the light of his truth on our faults, failures, and hang-ups can we begin to work on them.[28]

It is imperative that the white church give up racism and its sinful manifestations and join the black church in the struggle against oppression. Both can come together for the common good. When our nation is at war, we lay aside racial differences by sending and supporting both black and white soldiers on foreign land, but the church does not demonstrate this kind of collegiality at home. If blacks and whites can struggle together and give their lives against a foreign enemy, why can't black and white Christians struggle together at home against the domestic enemy called racism? The actions and commitment of both blacks and whites have conquered many foreign enemies, but our domestic enemy of racism is still unconquered. The reason is that the white church refuses to sanction war against it. Not only is this the shame of the nation, but also it is the shame of Western Christianity. James Cone asked, "Will [the church] continue its chaplaincy to the forces of oppression, or will it embrace the cause of liberation, proclaiming in word and deed the gospel of Christ?"[29]

To speak truth to power means the church cannot be identified with a system that has treated a people with contempt and marginalized them because of the color of their skin. The white church must identify with Christ and allow the Holy Spirit to renew it and set it free. Fred D. Wentzel wrote,

> There is no limit to what the church might accomplish if it should decide to take this action, and to belong in this respect to Christ and not to the world. Such a decision would mean more than the revival we so greatly need and so deeply desire; it would mean almost a new Pentecost. It would mean a release of spiritual power beyond our present dreams—power for the revitalizing of the church and for the healing of the nations. Renewals of life do not come cheaply, and this one would cost a searching of heart, a penitence, and a self-denying devotion to Christ on the part of Christians of both races far beyond anything the American church, at least, has known. But the solution of the racial issue, which threatens to destroy us, waits upon the church's becoming able to speak her own true word to the divided and warring races of mankind. For only a community which has itself become supernational and superracial has any chance of becoming the growing center of the universal human fellowship so desperately required.[30]

I hope the white church will undertake a serious examination of itself and repent and join Christ in the struggle for liberation and human dignity. I hope white readers don't view me as a hatemonger but rather as a person trying to bring two groups together for greater spiritual effectiveness and efficiency within the Body of Christ. I am by no means anti-white; I am anti-oppression, anti-racism, and anti-white supremacy. Christ worked against these things, and thus the white church must work against them as well. Whether those of the white church agree or disagree with this analysis, the fact remains that racism is alive and well in the church and the larger society. The violence and self-sabotage in inner cities and urban areas are the result of a system that has failed a people who got a late start in life and find it almost impossible to catch up. The cry that education and personal responsibility will improve the plight of an oppressed people is to some degree true, but to a larger degree if the system that has oppressed a people is not corrected, then education and personal responsibility will not change the outcome of a people. The American system needs correcting in order to level the playing field. In the words of Victor Hugo, "If a soul is left in darkness, sins will be committed. The guilty one is not he who commits the sin, but he who causes the darkness."[31] Unless the American system is corrected, America can never claim innocence for the despair and destruction that have flooded the streets of black America. Despite talk about education and personal responsibility, in which I completely believe, I cannot dismiss the responsibility of those who designed and created a system that has devastated a people, all with the rationalization and endorsement of the white church.

The White Church Must Help Correct the Oppressive System

Some whites may say they did not have a part in creating a system that has hurt and disfigured black people. The system was in place before their birth. What was done is in the past. I am not holding any one people accountable for what was created and done in the past. However, I can hold accountable those who benefit from the system but refuse to act in correcting it. As long as the system is set up so that one group receives the most of the best while another group receives the most of the worst, we can never say that our nation has reached economic, social, and political equality. The displacement of blacks after Hurricane Katrina is a prime example of a system that failed a people. Would this be the case if more of the hurricane victims were white? The system should work for all citizens, but it will not if the white church refuses to move against the spirit of racism. Whether one agrees with me or not, one cannot dismiss the cogent observation of Andrew Hacker:

> It is white America that has made being black so disconsolate an estate. Legal slavery may be in the past, but segregation and subordination have been allowed to persist. Even today, America imposes a stigma on every black child at birth. . . .
>
> A huge racial chasm remains, and there are few signs that the coming century will see it closed. A century and a quarter after slavery, white America continues to ask of its black citizens an extra patience and perseverance that whites have never required of themselves. So the question for white Americans is essentially moral: is it right to impose on members of an entire race a lesser start in life and then to expect from them a degree of resolution that has never been demanded from your own race?[32]

I believe our nation can be what it espouses to be. Much has been done to better our nation, but much more work remains. Howard Thurman wrote, "It is not enough to evict the devil; but something else must be put in his place and maintained there, or else he returns, refreshed and recharged, to deliver us over to a greater tyranny."[33] The struggle for justice and righteousness can never be relaxed because the forces of evil are always plotting to regain lost ground and rebuild what was torn down. I agree with Jon Nilson, who wrote to the white church and its theologians,

> To the extent that we white [Christians and theologians] fail to take an informed and active stand against racism, especially when it comes to engaging black theology, we will be working at cross purposes, contradicting our own self-designation as [Christians]. To this extent, we will give the people of our church good reason to question our credibility. If we are not visibly committed to achieving racial justice and to dismantling white privilege, what would keep us from being perceived as tolerant, if not actually supportive, of this nation's "original sin," which continues to benefit whites unjustly and to inflict real suffering on blacks? Why would it not seem that God, whose work and word we ponder, is really an idol, indifferent to black children's empty stomachs and crumbling classrooms, their parents' unemployment, substandard housing, and health care?[34]

Notes

1. H. Richard Niebuhr, *The Social Sources of Denominationalism* (New York: The World Publishing Company, 1957) 236–37. For the curse of Ham, see Genesis 9:20-27. This curse has been used by some to justify enslavement of people of black African ancestry because they were once believed to be descendants of Ham.

2. Amos Jones Jr., *Paul's Message of Freedom: What It Means to the Black Church* (Valley Forge PA: Judson Press, 1984) 131.

3. Cited in Howard Thurman, *The Luminous Darkness* (Richmond IN: Friends United Press, 1989) 55.

4. Fred D. Wentzel, *Epistle to White Christians* (Philadelphia: The Christian Education Press, 1948) 49.

5. James H. Cone, "The White Church and Black Power," in *Black Theology: A Documentary History, 1966–1979*, ed. Gayraud S. Wilmore and James H. Cone (New York: Orbis Book, 1979) 119.

6. Wentzel, *Epistle to White Christians*, 51.

7. Ibid., 56.

8. Joseph Barndt, *Dismantling Racism: The Continuing Challenge to White America* (Minneapolis: Augsburg, 1991) 29.

9. Andrew Hacker, *Two Nations Black and White, Separate, Hostile, Unequal* (New York: Ballantine Books, 1992, 1995) 33.

10. William R. Jones, "Purpose and Method in Liberation Theology: Implication for an Interim Assessment," in *Liberation Theology: North American Style*, ed. Deane William Ferm (New York: Vertizon, 1987) 152–53.

11. Hacker, *Two Nations Black and White*, 65.

12. E. Franklin Frazier, *Black Bourgeoisie* (New York: Collier Books, 1965) 115.

13. William R. Jones, *Is God a White Racist?* (New York: Anchor Press/Doubleday, 1973) 77.

14. Hacker, *Two Nations Black and White*, 66.

15. Niebuhr, *The Social Sources of Denominationalism*, 259–60.

16. Paul Rogat Loeb, *Soul of a Citizen: Living with Conviction in a Cynical Time* (New York: St. Martin's Griffin, 1999) 4.

17. Report of the National Advisory Commission on Civil Disorder, U.S. Government Printing Office, 1968, p. 1.

18. Martin Luther King Jr., "Letter from the Birmingham Jail," in *A Testament of Hope: The Essential Writings of Martin Luther King, Jr.*, ed. James Melvin Washington (San Francisco: Harper & Row, Publishers, 1986) 295.

19. Paulo Freire, *Pedagogy of the Oppressed* (New York: Herder & Herder, 1970) 35.

20. Wentzel, *Epistle to White Christians*, 91.

21. Cain Hope Felder, *Troubling Biblical Waters* (New York: Orbis Books, 1989) 37.

22. Frank M. Snowden, *Before Color Prejudice* (Cambridge MA: Harvard University Press, 1983) 73.

23. Cited in Frank M. Snowden, *Blacks in Antiquity* (Cambridge MA: Harvard University Press, 1970) 196.

24. Ibid., 196.

25. Charles B. Copher, "Three Thousand Years of Biblical Interpretation with Reference to Black People," *Journal of the Interdenominational Theological Center* 30/2 (Spring 1986): 124.

26. John L. Johnson, *The Black Biblical Heritage* (St. Louis MO: Black Biblical Heritage Publishing Company, 1988) 151.

27. Cited in Gyasi A. Foluke, *The Real Holocaust: A Wholistic Analysis of the African-American Experience, 1441–1994* (New York: Carlton Press Corporation, 1995) 392.

28. Rick Warren, *The Purpose Driven Life* (Grand Rapids MI: Zondervan, 2002) 220.

29. James H. Cone, "The White Church and Black Power," 131.

30. Wentzel, *Epistle to White Christians*, 90–91.

31. Cited in *A Testament of Hope*, ed. James Melvin Washington, 192.

32. Andrew Hacker, *Two Nations Black and White*, 245.

33. Howard Thurman, *Deep Is the Hunger* (Richmond IN: Friends United Press, 1951) 52.

34. Jon Nilson, *Hearing Past the Pain: Why White Catholic Theologians Need Black Theology* (New York/Mahwah NJ: Paulist Press, 2007) 66.

Discussion Questions

1. The author notes that the church "has been divided for centuries across racial lines." Visualize your congregation. Are all the faces similar, or are there people of various ethnic backgrounds? If your church is relatively homogeneous, how do you think people would react to a visitor from a different background? Why do you think churches are still so segregated, even when they claim to be otherwise?

_____

_____

_____

_____

2. In general, how do you think the white church has responded to the plight of black Americans? Do you think white people have any level of responsibility toward their black brothers and sisters in Christ?

_____

_____

_____

_____

3. The author states, "blacks do not practice racism, for racism relates to power dynamics that blacks do not possess." Do you agree with his statement and his reasoning? What is the difference between racism and prejudice? How might either attitude hinder the progress of Christ's church?

_____

_____

_____

_____

4. In the section titled "Racism Is Not an Ancient Phenomenon," the author explores the origins of racism. Why did people come to regard each other based on skin color? How do whites sometimes rationalize their negative perceptions of blacks? What Scriptures might they cite to support their views? What counter Scriptures can you cite?

_____

_____

_____

_____

5. It is likely that the schism between whites and blacks will remain unless people from both sides take positive steps toward reconciliation and healing. Can you think of some practical steps the people in your church, whether white or black, could take to change racial perceptions? What could your church to do improve the plight of blacks in the area where you live?

_____

_____

_____

_____

Chapter 5

FUTURE LEADERSHIP OF THE BLACK CHURCH

To pray for justice without analyzing the causes of injustice is to turn religion into an opium of the people. The time has come for the black church to take a critical look at its vision with the intention of radically changing its priorities.

—James H. Cone

Not an Impossible Mission

One day I saw a movie called *Mission Impossible* in which Tom Cruise was the main actor. The movie was about the mission of exposing and eradicating corruption and highlighted the difficulty involved in accomplishing this goal. However, Tom Cruise was successful in accomplishing his mission. Thus, the title of the movie—*Mission Impossible*—confused me. The title conveys that the mission is impossible to accomplish. Impossible means incapable of being done; it means something cannot be changed or corrected regardless of what we do. Yet, in the movie the mission is accomplished. Then I realized the movie is teaching the church a great lesson: though something seems impossible—though it seems useless to try to change or correct it—the mission can be accomplished when we act together and never allow ourselves to believe we fight a losing battle. We have lost many battles by depending more on our cognitive perceptions of impossibility than on our faith in ourselves and God, and this prohibits us from facing and dealing with the acute crisis in black America. We still walk by sight and not by faith. Our problems have become like giants, and we view ourselves as grasshoppers.

What we see in our communities, society, and the nation as a whole horrifies us. We see all kinds of social, economic, and psychological problems. We see depressing instances of broken families, unemployment, homicides, incarceration, diseases, out of wedlock pregnancies, high school dropouts, crime and drugs, police brutality, and a host of other problems. When we consider these enormous social problems, we act as if our mission is impossible, and we stand by watching these events unfold before our eyes without trying to get involved to change the present situation. Our churches have become havens for escapism. We are more concerned about accommodating than we are about transforming our world. We are more concerned about avoiding confrontations with the power structure than we are about the hurting people in the world. We bury ourselves behind stained-glass windows because we are afraid to tackle the giant problems within our communities.

It is a known fact that black people stay in church the longest, but they have the most problems. Are we trying to worship and praise God into doing for us what we can do for ourselves? Have we forgotten God's words spoken by the prophet Amos? "I hate, I despise your festivals, and I take no delight in your solemn assemblies. . . . Take away from me the noise of your songs; I will not listen to the melody of your harps. But let justice roll down like waters, and righteousness like an ever flowing stream" (5:21, 23-24, RSV). We cannot preach, sing, and shout our problems away while black America sinks in a quagmire, families shatter, black rage is at the point of explosion, prisons burst at the seams, jobs are scarce, and young people are caught within a subculture of violence. Sunday worship is fine, but "A Christian hasn't finished his job when he has gone to [worship] on Sunday. The church's prayers, the body of Christ, are only given as a help towards bringing [the Christian] to the world. And if [people] do not recognize in us the love and goodness of our Father, then we have done nothing—we haven't even begun to serve Him."[1] Our mission is not impossible, and we must do much more if the black church is to be relevant in the twenty-first century.

We Didn't Pay Attention

Robert N. Bellah concludes his book *The Good Society* with a powerful chapter called "Democracy Means Paying Attention."[2] He and his colleagues remind us to pay attention to the institutions that shape us. In terms of urban black communities, black America stopped paying attention to the mounting crisis. After the civil rights struggle, black America in general and the black church in particular got distracted from our focus on the next generation. When desegregation occurred and there was a middle class exodus out of many black communities, we stopped paying attention. When we became the first blacks in this position and in that position, we stopped paying attention. When our buying power increased year after year, we stopped paying attention. While many of us enjoyed our newfound freedom and anemic privileges, we stopped paying attention. As a result of not paying attention, our standards started to erode; the next generation formed their own cultural norms; our youth started dropping out of high school; and our children started to have children. When we stopped paying attention, sexual predators started snatching and molesting our daughters. Because we stopped paying attention, drugs and handguns flooded our streets, and families started falling apart. Due to distractions, new forms of nihilism hem us in. Our crisis situation means the black church can no longer afford to stop paying attention. "Paying attention is how we use our psychic energy, and how we use our psychic energy determines the kind of self we are cultivating, the kind of person we are learning to be. . . . The nature of the institutions we both inhabit and transform has much to do with our capacity to sustain attention."[3] The urgency of the times calls for the black church to pay attention and put its energy and resources into stabilizing and liberating the black community.

The Need for a New Consciousness

This century calls for blacks to develop a new consciousness so they can employ new models, approaches, thinking, actions, risks, and sacrifices to turn around lives headed for mayhem and destruction. Without a new consciousness, blacks will commit genocide, for their current consciousness does not motivate them to do for themselves. Instead, they enrich others while impoverishing themselves. The black church must encourage blacks to develop their own consciousness, for this the only way to empower the poor and oppressed. They need the tools, training, and temerity to lift themselves out of socioeconomic degradation. The black church must focus it gaze on the people and take the necessary steps to help them (e.g., encouraging education, creating literacy programs, reinforcing moral standards, uplifing blacks' contributions worldwide, teaching and demonstrating fiscal responsibility, encouraging black business, mentoring youth). It must struggle with the people against institutional structures that stifle their movement toward liberation. Spiritualizing oppression is no longer acceptable. The oppressed must be empowered to struggle for their needs and not manipulated to relegate liberation to a future event.

Currently, the black church is not creating a revolutionary spirit in the people to transform their situation. James Cone stated,

> Forgetting their reason for existing, the black churches [are], as Washington appropriately describes, "amusement centers," "arenas for power politics," and an "organ for recognition, leadership, and worship." They [are] perversions of the gospel of Christ and places for accommodating the oppressed plight of black people.[4]

With all the social, economic, and educational problems of the black community, it is sad that many churches have turned into entertainment centers in which preachers are bartenders giving people intoxicating drinks of prosperity and materialism, and feeding them the stale bread of ease and comfort. To manipulate the people into thinking all they have to do is "name it and claim it" without teaching them to live within their means and reduce their consumerism only furthers their misery and oppression. Billions of dollars flow through the collective hands of black America. Unfortunately, the money benefits not the black community but those who produce products that target the black community for consumption. Black Americans will always be at the bottom of the economic ladder until they develop a new consciousness that motivates them to invest in themselves and stop the outflow of their dollars to empower other ethnic groups. Black Americans need to be taught how to be wise investors. They need to be taught not to buy what they want and then beg for what they need. Money management and investment are two major issues facing black Americans. Money serves whatever is in the consciousness, and this is the why a new consciousness is desperately needed.

Twelve Things Blacks Must Do

In the early twentieth century, Nannie Helen Burroughs highlighted twelve things black Americans must do for themselves. I think the black church must aggressively teach and preach these twelve things along with the gospel of liberation to help improve the plight of the race. Burroughs's points are sadly as relevant today as they were when she first wrote them.

1. The Negro must learn to put first-things first. The first things are education; development of character traits; a trade and home ownership. The Negro puts too much of his earning in clothes, food, in show and having what he calls "A good time." Dr. Kelly Miller said, "The Negro buys what he wants and begs for what he needs."

2. The Negro must stop expecting God and white folk to do for him what he can do for himself. It is the "Divine Plan" that the strong shall help the weak, but even God does not do for man what man can do for himself. The Negro will have to do exactly what Jesus told the man (in John 5:8) to do—Carry his own load—"Take up your bed and walk."

3. The Negro must keep himself, his children, and his home clean and make the surroundings in which he lives comfortable and attractive. He must learn to "Run his community up"—not down. We can segregate by law; we integrate only by living. Civilization is not a matter of race, it is a matter of standards.

4. The Negro must learn to dress more appropriately for work and for leisure. Knowing what to wear—how to wear it—when to wear it and where to wear it, are earmarks of common sense, culture, and also an index to character.

5. The Negro must make his religion an everyday practice and not just a Sunday go to meeting emotional affair.

6. The Negro must highly resolve to wipe out mass ignorance. The leaders of the race must teach and inspire the masses to become eager and determined to improve mentally, morally, and spiritually, and to meet the basic requirements of good citizenship. We should initiate an intensive literacy campaign in America, as well, as in Africa. Ignorance—satisfied ignorance—is a millstone about the neck of the race. It is democracy's greatest burden.

7. The Negro must stop charging his failure to his color and to white people's attitude. The truth of the matter is that good service and conduct will make senseless race prejudice fade like mist before a rising sun. God never intended that a man's color shall be anything other than a badge of distinction. It is high time that all races were learning that fact. The Negro

must first Qualify for whatever position he want. Purpose, initiative, ingenuity, and industry are the keys that all [people] use to get what they want. The Negro will have to do the same. He must make himself a workman who is too skilled not to be wanted, and too Dependable not to be on the job, according to promise or plan. He will never become a vital factor in industry until he learns to put into his work the vitalizing force of initiative, skill, and dependability. He has gone "Rights" mad and "Duty" dumb.

8. The Negro must overcome his bad job habits. He must make a brand new reputation for himself in the world of labor. His bad job habits are absenteeism, funerals to attend, or a little business to look after. The Negro runs an off and on business. He also has a bad reputation for conduct on the job—such as petty quarrelling with other help, incessant loud talking about nothing; loafing, carelessness, due to lack of job pride; insolence, gum chewing and—too often—liquor drinking. Just plain bad job habits!

9. He must improve his conduct in public places. Taken as a whole, he is entirely too loud and too ill-mannered. There is much talk about wiping out racial segregation and also talk about achieving integration. Segregation is a physical arrangement by which people are separated in various services. It is definitely up to the Negro to wipe out the apparent justification or excuse for segregation. The only effective way to do it is to clean up and keep clean. By practice, cleanliness will become a habit and habit becomes character.

10. The Negro must learn how to operate business for people—not for Negro people only. To do business, he will have to remove all typical "earmarks," business principles; measure up to accepted standards and meet stimulating competition, graciously—in fact, he must learn to welcome competition.

11. The average so-called educated Negro will have to come down out of the air. He is too inflated over nothing. He needs an experience similar to the one that Ezekiel had—(Ezekiel 3:14-19). And he must do what Ezekiel did. Otherwise, through indifference, as to the plight of the masses, the Negro who think that he has escaped, will lose his soul. . . . A race transforms itself through its own leaders and its sensible "common people." A race rises on its own wings, or is held down by its own weight. True leaders are never "things apart from the people." They are the masses. They simply got to the front ahead of them. Their only business at the front is to inspire the masses by hard work and noble example and challenge them to "Come on!" Dante stated a fact when he said, "Show the people the light and they will find the way!"

12. The Negro must stop forgetting his friends. Read Deuteronomy 24:18. Deuteronomy rings the big bell of gratitude. Why? Because an ingrate is an abomination in the sight of God. God is constantly telling us that "I the Lord thy God delivered you"—through human instrumentalities. The American Negro had and still has friends—in the North and in the South. These friends not only pray, speak, write, influence others, but make unbelievable, unpublished sacrifices and contributions for the advancement of the race—for their brothers in bonds. The noblest thing that the Negro can do is to live and labor that these benefactors will not have given in vain. The Negro must make his heart warm with gratitude, his lips sweet with thanks and his heart and mind resolute with purpose to justify the sacrifices and stand on his feet and go forward—"God is no respector of persons. In every nation, he that feareth him and worketh righteousness is" sure to win out. Get to work! That's the answer to everything that hurts us. We talk too much about nothing instead of redeeming the time by working. Remember, In spite of race prejudice, America is brim full of opportunities. Go after them![5]

I do not suggest that all blacks are implicated in not doing what Nannie Helen Burroughs highlighted. I acknowledge that many blacks have done and are doing what she suggested and more. Even so, a large percentage of blacks are not living wisely, making wise decisions, and spending wisely. When we see a large percentage of the race, especially among our youth, who are not taught to practice core values, we need to revisit, discuss, and practice Burrough's twelve things. These core values can help raise the standards of a people. The moral standards in black America are too low. The black church may not be able to solve all the problems, but it can hold up a standard before the people. The black church must be the example it wishes to see in the community it serves. The lack of decorum, respect, and dignity in black America, especially among black youth, is appalling. Many children and young adults don't know how to read and write, which is a major impediment to their social and economic progress now and in the future. The black church has to find a way to start over again, teaching and preaching core vales, etiquette, and ethics to improve the race whose children are far behind the rest of the nation.

We Must Concentrate on Our Youth

The progress of a people depends on the stabilization of the family and how well their youth are prepared for the future. In many ways, we are failing our youth. We must change the culture and values of our youth; otherwise, they will perish before the eyes of the generation that spurned them. One of the problems is that too many parents are not truly parenting their children. Many parents want to be their children's friends rather than their parents. There is plenty of time for children to gain friends. What they need are parents who love them, discipline them, and set boundaries for them. Love is not boundless. Inherent within love are boundaries. Setting boundaries for children is an expression of love to help them not harm themselves and cut their lives short. Without setting boundaries, it is difficult if not impossible to raise children and make demands on them. Howard Thurman wrote,

> One of the reasons our age is so beset by the behavior of its youth lies in the fact that we have lost the ability to make demands on them an ultimate challenge to all their powers. No one likes to be asked to do what he can do too easily; this is the other side of the coin. The glory of any challenge is the fact that it is a challenge. We have only contempt, in the end, for the task that requires no real effort.[6]

Our children can learn, but they must be challenged, and the black church must help create a culture free of the crime, violence, and fear that currently keep our children from obtaining a strong education. When children struggle against their toxic environment while trying to get an education, the odds are so stacked against them that few make it. Janice Hale-Benson believes "[b]lack children do not enter school disadvantaged. They emerge from school as disadvantaged youth. For this reason the church must evaluate its ministries to black youth based in part on an accurate assessment of the core causes of the challenges they face. It necessitates confronting the difficulties children and youth experience in negotiating the school."[7]

As difficult as it may be, the church must continue to struggle against oppression and the low expectation of our youth. Accepting low to mediocre standards is not an option. We must create an atmosphere of excellence in morality, education, and personal responsibility. The black church must find ways to strengthen the black family and encourage parents to get involved in the education of their children. Often, parents only react when children fail, get in trouble or do something reprehensible that affects their education. Too many parents are reactive instead of proactive in working with the schools to catch problems early enough to do something about them. Bill Cosby rightly said,

What we need now is parents sitting down with children, overseeing homework, sending children off to school in the morning, well-fed, clothed, rested, and ready to learn . . . change can only be set in motion when families and leaders get together and acknowledge that a problem exists. Where are the standards that tell a child: "Stop! There is hope." This has to happen in the home. It reverts back to parenting.[8]

Juan Williams says Bill Cosby's challenge to black people, especially black parents,

is a call to arms for black people to stop waiting for the end of "systemic racism" or for more money for schools. A black child born today will be old or dead long before the end of racism or before a time when every public school is successfully reformed. America is now at the point where giving hope to black children is a radical idea. It is radical to speak against an anti-educational mindset and in favor of reclaiming the black heritage of making education the heart of the struggle for racial equality.[9]

Parental involvement in children's education is a key factor in children's success. High achievers among black children and youth often attribute their ambition to their parents' expectations and involvement with their education. Our children can rise to high expectations. Although there are many shortfalls of the schools, "the black church has served and must continue to serve in the area of self-concept development, leadership development, and the projection of positive role models for black children and youth. . . . [T]he church must continue to serve as an arena for achievement in developing speaking skills, skills in the expressive arts and co-curricular activities that enrich academic achievement."[10]

The black church must continue to reach out and support our youth and those who are unchurched and irreligious. We must recognize the possibilities in reaching the lost and overcoming the forces against the oppressed. Doing so requires commitment from homes, churches, and school systems. Commitment is key in lifting up a downtrodden people. However, even if no other institution makes the commitment to our youth, the church must. Otherwise the few who are in the church will also leave the pews. Carter G. Woodson stated, "The young people of the Negro race could be held in the church . . . , but the Negro's Christianity does not conceive of social uplift as a duty of the church; and consequently Negro children have not been adequately trained in religious matters to be equal to the social demands upon them."[11] Until the black church develops a theology of economic, social, and political action, it will not retain loyal worshipers. If the content of the black church does not reflect the social context in which the people live out their lives, the church will remain irrelevant.

Orthodoxy and Orthopraxy

If our Christian claim is authentic, the creeds and the deeds of the black church must join together. The black church preaches and teaches that Jesus rose from the dead and gives us power to overcome the same forces that tried to defeat him. If the black church truly believes this, then its actions ought to be no less than the actions of Jesus who motivated the oppressed to think and act differently than the way they were taught, and to struggle against oppression. Jesus' mission is not impossible. Too often we act like the unbelieving children of Israel who were in close proximity to the promised land when fear and unfaithfulness caused them to retreat and wander in the wilderness. In a similar vein, the black church has retreated and is wandering around in America, fearful, unorganized, and unprepared to meet new challenges. While we have church instead of being the church, our children are crying and dying, and hopelessness and dread have caked our feet and actions to the point that we are increasingly becoming irrelevant. This sluggard attitude must be broken to overcome our frightening situation. It seems the black church is satisfied with its buildings, conferences, and programs while black America perishes across this nation. The black church must reorder its priorities and practice what it preaches.

Divine Dissatisfaction

Why is there no outcry from the black church that produces the kind of revolutionary action needed to bring about transformation? Where is our "divine dissatisfaction"? Martin Luther King Jr. stated,

> [We must] be dissatisfied until the tragic walls that separate the outer city of wealth and comfort and the inner city of poverty and despair shall be crushed by the battering rams of the forces of justice. [We must] be dissatisfied until those that live on the outskirts of hope are brought into the metropolis of daily security. [We must] be dissatisfied until slums are cast into the junk heaps of history, and every family is living in a decent sanitary home.[12]

The black church is too satisfied, too complacent, too apathetic, and too otherworldly. Unless we become dissatisfied and create the kind of revolutionary action that moves against oppression, black nihilism, joblessness, and disunity, the prognosis for black America in the future is dim. We have an enormous job ahead us, and we must put all of our energy and resources into hating what God hates and loving what God loves. Having church is not enough. What do we do after the benediction is given? In most cases, we return home until the next worship service. When are we going to move from merely worshiping to actually practicing the faith? Our duty is to "turn seekers into saints, turn consumers into contributors, turn members into ministers [of disciples], and turn an audience into an army"[13] so we can combat the forces that are destroying the social fabric of our community and the nation. We cannot afford to be satisfied anymore. Satisfaction is one of the reasons people view the church as irrelevant. We have made peace with the way things are. To fight the good fight of faith is not to be satisfied with the way things are. History reveals that social changes have come about through the dissatisfaction of people. We must develop the kind of dissatisfaction that produces struggle. Frederick Douglass stated, "This struggle may be a moral one, or it may be a physical one, and it may be both moral and physical, but it must be a struggle. Power concedes nothing without a demand. It never did and it never will."[14]

New Leadership for the Twenty-first Century

This century requires new moral and focused leadership. We need leaders who will consistently speak out and struggle against unjust social and political structures. The transformation of black America and the nation as a whole cannot happen without morally strong, committed leadership. The black church must develop and produce leaders who are full of the Holy Spirit, well trained, and not afraid of controversy, public attacks, and ridicule because they are working for the liberation of their communities. Too often church leaders avoid being controversial because they don't want to disturb the status quo. They want their peers and society to speak well of them. They are more concerned about popularity than they are about being prophetic. But these leaders forget the words of Jesus: "Woe to you, when all men speak well of you, for so their fathers did to the false prophets" (Luke 6:26, RSV). Church leaders know that "[t]he religion of Jesus, applied to modern society, is revolutionary. But with professional success at stake, most of [them] are afraid to be radical."[15]

The words of Bruce Catton can be applied to many church leaders today: "They play everything safe, preach only on subjects that never reach the level of live controversy, and cuddle up to their members, their boards, and the powers-that-be in the hope of enjoying an untroubled and prosperous senescence."[16] Leaders of the church must understand that Jesus never played it safe. His ministry was controversial; he was a victim of people's attacks and under constant surveillance, but he was not afraid to speak out and struggle against injustice. He demonstrated over and over again that he came to serve not pacify people. He came to bring a sword not peace on earth. He said, "For I have come to set a man against his father, and a daughter against her mother, and a daughter-in-law against her mother-in-law; and a man's foes will be those of his own household" (Matt 10:35, RSV). There was and is nothing weak and compromising about Jesus. He rocked the boat for justice and righteousness. We must do likewise if we are going to transform our present times. When we stand up against what is wrong and unjust, we will be persecuted. Jesus said, "A disciple is not above his teacher, nor a servant above his master; it is enough for the disciple to be like his teacher, and the servant like his master. If they have called the master of the house Be-el'zebul, how much more will they malign those of his household" (Matt 10:24-25, RSV). Jesus was not afraid of controversy or of being radical, and if we follow Jesus Christ we should not be afraid either.

The crisis facing black America is so critical that there is no question that in the twenty-first century, the black church needs new informed leaders who can strategize, communicate, and motivate the oppressed to rock the boat for justice and righteousness. We need leaders who will take seriously the words of one of our great predecessors, Frederick Douglass, who encouraged a new generation to "Agitate! Agitate! Agitate!" Wherever there is wrong, agitate. Wherever there is evil, agitate. Wherever there is injustice, agitate. The black church must agitate not accommodate until it has transformed the present situation into the kingdom of God. Part of the reason the church is ineffective and increasingly becoming irrelevant is that it accommodates rather than agitates. Accommodation of evil and injustice does not build up the church and community. Christopher Lasch makes a cogent observation of how accommodation affects our democracy, which can also be said to affect the church as well.

> It is our reluctance to make demands on each other, much more than our reluctance to help those in need, that is sapping the strength of democracy today. We have become far too accommodating and tolerant for our own

good. In the name of sympathetic understanding, we tolerate second-rate standards of personal conduct. We put up with bad manners and with many kinds of bad language, ranging from the commonplace scatology that is now ubiquitous to elaborate academic evasion. We seldom bother to correct a mistake or to argue with opponents in the hope of changing their minds. Instead we either shout them down or agree to disagree, saying that all of us have a right to our opinions. . . . Tolerance and understanding are important virtues, but they must not become an excuse for apathy.[17]

The black church must agitate because people cannot move toward their liberation until they do so. Through this agitation process, the oppressed will come to know who they are and identify the forces that oppress them. Once they are enlightened through this process of agitation, they can struggle to restore their humanity and restore hope in the future. Leadership of the black church must encourage unification and agitation of the status quo, and also be critical of the actions of the oppressed that often work at cross-purposes with their liberation.

From Survival to Liberation

Church leadership in the twenty-first century must work to help move the black church beyond a survival model of operation to a liberation model of operation. The black church has not yet made this paradigm shift. It still operates from a survival mode. By surviving, I mean trying to exist by paying the church bills, making it to the next church anniversary, and avoiding addressing and meeting the pressing needs of the community. We are at a point in history in which it will take more than mere survival. Our slave foreparents survived, making a way for us to continue the struggle for total liberation. To reach total liberation, there must be a new mindset and strategy to bring about fundamental changes in the lives of people who are oppressed. Again, the goal is to empower the people to act on behalf of their own self-interest. Cornel West makes a significant point concerning the direction and leadership of the black church:

The black church is going to have to change in order to meet new challenges. Its leadership is going to have to become much more sophisticated, critical and self-critical. This is the only way that democratic sensibilities can become more pronounced and pervasive in the black community. Second, it has to become more grounded in intellectual inquiry. We can no longer have leaders who engage simply and primarily in putting forth moral condemnation and ethical rhetoric without any understanding of how power and wealth operate in this society.[18]

To achieve total liberation, the black church leadership must emphasize infrastructure within the black community. Without an economic infrastructure in the black community, black people can never develop the kind of social and political power needed to bring about transformation. The vision of the black church must be broader, more well defined, and have commonality that black Americans can embrace across class and economic lines. Leaders must push the idea for self-reliance if the people are to love themselves and believe they can be free and independent. Leaders must challenge people out of their "learned helplessness" and encourage them to be as resourceful and competitive as other ethnic groups such as Jewish and Japanese Americans. Black America must unlearn their socialized self-hatred if they are to be as successful as other racial groups. Amos Wilson stated,

> If the institutional Black Church is to realize its and the Black community's economic potential, if it is to maximize its ability to realize its spiritual mission and to meet the material needs of the community which so desperately depends on its leadership and stewardship, it must remedy what Lincoln refers to as "one of the major weakness of the historic Black denominations . . . the lack of the training and teaching of their denominational leaders, pastors, and laity about all aspects of economic stewardship, from careful record keeping, financial accountability, and investments to the economic development of their communities." Training and consciousness-raising in these areas must take place in the schools as well as in the local churches and community educational institutions.[19]

Participation in Liberation

Visionary leaders must persuade the people to participate in their liberation. They must say no to oppression, exploitation, and marginalization. Leaders must challenge a people not to solely depend on government social programs, which are useful in giving a hand up but not a constant handout. A people cannot reach social and economic self-sufficiency through constant handouts. People who have been demoralized for centuries due to oppression need a helping hand up, but constant handouts can keep the oppressed in a state of powerlessness. The oppressed must be careful not to be forever caught in the manipulation of welfare programs. Paulo Freire said "welfare

programs as instruments of manipulation ultimately serve the end of con-
quest. They act as an anesthetic, distracting the oppressed from the true
causes of their problem and from the concrete solution of these problems."[20]
We need leaders who can see through the manipulations of an oppressive
system and expose them, working with the poor and oppressed in an effort
to wean them off this kind of system. The cycle of dependency must be
broken, and the church must help to create employment for the people that
would give them dignity and self-respect. Working with and teaching the
people self-reliance is the responsibility of both the church and community
leaders. Participation in liberation will help the people decide their own des-
tinies and not let someone else decide it for them. Leaders must preach and
teach the people that they hold the power to cancel their collective misery.

Jesus Christ Our Example

Future leaders must be truly and deeply committed to the social, economic,
and political uplift of the people. What made Jesus such an effective leader is
that he stayed within the great prophetic tradition; he confronted groups
with power that oppressed and exploited the weak, and he worked with the
oppressed, empowering them to advance not the interest of the Roman
Empire but the kingdom of God. Jesus' whole ministry was based upon lifting up the downtrodden, recovering the sight of the blind, and setting free
those help captive. Yes, he was controversial. Yes, he was radical. Yes, he was
not politically correct. Yes, he was a threat to the power structure. Yes, he was
maligned and criticized, but he never wavered from his commitment to God
and the people. Jesus Christ is our ultimate example. His leadership sets the
standard for the church. We cannot correct the problem by going alone with
what is; we correct unjust situations by struggling against them. Jesus didn't
go along to get along. He didn't compromise with wrong, evil, and injustice.
He challenged these things, and we must do likewise. Too many church leaders go along to get along because they don't want to upset their constituency,
believing this might cause an economic and social backlash. These leaders are
more concerned about respectability than they are about responsibility. Like
Jesus, leaders must be responsible to God first and then to the people, but
never become priests to the status quo. To change and correct the plight of
suffering people, black church leadership must model themselves after Jesus
Christ. It is then necessary for the black church to demand the kind of leadership that Jesus demonstrated as relevant for the twenty-first century. We

must fervently pray for leaders like Jesus Christ. To paraphrase the words of Josiah G. Holland,

> God give us leaders! A time like this demands
> Strong minds, great hearts, true faith, and ready hands,
> Leaders whom the lust of office does not kill;
> Leaders whom the spoils of life cannot buy
> Leaders who possess opinions and a will;
> Leaders who have honor; Leaders who will not lie!
> Leaders who can stand before a demagogue
> And damn his treacherous flatteries without winking;
> Tall Leaders, sun crowned, who live above the fog
> In public duty and in private thinking;
> For while the rabble with their thumb-worn creeds,
> Their large profession and their little deeds
> Mingle in a selfish strife, lo! Freedom weeps,
> Wrong rules the land, and waiting Justice sleeps.[21]

Notes

1. Cited in James H. Cone, *Black Theology and Black Power* (New York: Orbis Books, 1997) 129.

2. Robert N. Bellah, *The Good Society* (New York: Knopf/Random House, 1991).

3. Cited in Cornel West, *Prophetic Reflections: Notes on Race and Power in America* (Monroe ME: Common Courage Press, 1993) 201.

4. Cone, *Black Theology and Black Power*, 106.

5. Nannie Helen Burroughs, *12 Things the Negro Must Do for Himself*, c. early 1900s, out of print. See Karen Hunter, *Who Are You Calling Niggardly? Seven Things Blacks Need to Stop Worrying About and Twelve Things the Negro Must Do* (New York: Pocket Books, 2010).

6. Howard Thurman, *Disciplines of the Spirit* (Richmond IN: Friends United Press, 1987) 30–31.

7. Janice Hale-Benson, "Psychosocial Experiences," in *Working with Black Youth: Opportunities for Christian Ministry*, ed. Charles R. Foster & Grant S. Shockley (Nashville: Abingdon Press, 1989) 34.

8. Cited in Juan Williams, *Enough* (New York: Three Rivers Press, 2006) 105.

9. Ibid., 105.

10. Hale-Benson, "Psychosocial Experiences," 49.

11. Carter G. Woodson, *Miseducation of the Negro* (Washington DC: The Associated Publishers, 1969) 69.

12. Martin Luther King Jr., "Where Do We Go From Here," in *A Testament of Hope*, ed. James Melvin Washington (San Francisco: Harper & Row Publishers, 1986) 251.

13. Rick Warren, *The Purpose Driven Church* (Grand Rapids MI: Zondervan, 1995) 367.

14. John Blassingame, *The Frederick Douglass Papers*, series 3, *Speeches, Debates, and Interviews*, vol. 3, 1855–1863 (New Haven: Yale University Press, 1985) 204.

15. Daniel D. Walker, *The Human Problems of the Minister* (New York: Harper & Row, Publishers, 1960) 143.

16. Cited in Walker, *The Human Problems of the Minister*, 146.

17. Christopher Lasch, *The Revolt of the Elites and the Betrayal of Democracy* (New York: W. W. Norton & Company, 1995) 107.

18. Cornel West, *Prophetic Reflections: Notes on Race and Power in America* (Monroe ME: Common Courage Press, 1993) 73.

19. Amos Wilson, *Blueprint for Black Power: A Moral, Political, and Economic Imperative for the Twenty-first Century* (New York: Afrikan World InfoSystems, 1998) 574–75.

20. Paulo Freire, *Pedagogy of the Oppressed* (New York: Continuum Publishing Company, 1999) 133.

21. Cited in *Light from Many Lamps*, ed. Lillian E. Watson (New York: Simon & Schuster, 1951) 183.

Discussion Questions

1. Name what you perceive as the three biggest problems facing black Americans today. What is the church's responsibility in addressing these problems? How is the church shirking its role in the lives of blacks?

_____

_____

_____

_____

2. Can you think of black churches that have taken positive steps to help? How have they improved someone's circumstances? What gifts do members of your congregation possess that could aid in creating support groups, clinics, after-school opportunities, clothes closets, food banks, or other programs?

_____

_____

_____

_____

3. The author lists Nannie Helen Burroughs's "Twelve Things Blacks Must Do," which she wrote in the early 1900s as a commentary on the ways black people could improve their circumstances. How relevant, practical, and doable are these items today?

_____

_____

_____

_____

4. The author quotes Janice Hale-Benson, who believes "[b]lack children do not enter school disadvantaged. They emerge from school as disadvantaged youth. For this reason the church must evaluate its ministries to black youth based in part on an accurate assessment of the core causes of the challenges they face. It necessitates confronting the difficulties children and youth experience in negotiating the school." List the difficulties encountered by the black children in your community. What is the church's role in helping these young people, and how can the church attract more young families?

_____

_____

_____

_____

5. Jesus Christ, the author insists, is our "ultimate example." He was controversial, radical, politically incorrect, a threat to the power structure, and maligned and criticized. However, he "never wavered from his commitment to God and the people." Search the Gospels for ways Jesus went against cultural expectations to care for someone in need. How can his example encourage us as we discern the best ways to help liberate black Americans?

_____

_____

_____

_____

Chapter 6

WE NEED
THE HOLY SPIRIT

But, you will receive power when the Holy Spirit has come upon you; and you will be my witnesses in Jerusalem, in all Judea and Samaria, and to the ends of the earth.

—Acts 1:8, RSV

What Is the Holy Spirit?

The Holy Spirit is the force or power Christ promised to send the disciples to aid and comfort them in carrying out the mandates of the gospel. It is considered the third person of the Trinity that works in the heart of believers to guide and guard them. It is a gift to the church to nurture and empower its people for the kingdom of God. In order for the postmodern church to be effective in the twenty-first century, it must have the Holy Spirit. The Holy Spirit was sent to the early church not for amusement but for empowerment. The Holy Spirit confirms and affirms what Christ has done for humanity, and it is available for us to carry on the work Christ started centuries ago. Today too many churches emphasize prosperity and materialism instead of the indwelling presence of the Holy Spirit, which is a must if we are to redeem the evil times in which we live. The Holy Spirit not only transforms us but also equips us to do God's good will and purpose. The confusion, conflict, and contradictions we find in the church and among Christians are the direct result of the absence of the indwelling of the Holy Spirit. Without the Holy Spirit, our churches are nothing more than entertainment centers; people leave them the same way they came in. Emotionalism does not mean the presence of the Holy Spirit. Emotionalism does not transform hearts and characters. The Holy Spirit does this. This is the reason worship must be done in Spirit and in truth in order for God's people to conquer the strong addictions of the flesh. The powers and principalities that hold God's people captive can never be broken unless the Holy Spirit breaks them. We can never lift communities out of their deep and destructive malaise unless the Holy Spirit dwells in and through us. It doesn't matter how well trained, educated, and degreed we are; it doesn't matter how many fields of specificity we can boast; it doesn't matter how many churches exist in the community; we will never be able to transform today's narcissistic culture without the Holy Spirit.

Knowledge Is Not Enough

Some say we need more knowledge to transform our times. Our resources should be designated for acquiring more knowledge. There is no doubt that knowledge is a valuable tool in solving the problems of our times, but, as T. S. Eliot asked, "Where is the knowledge that is lost in information? Where is the wisdom that is lost in knowledge?"[1] Knowledge alone is not enough. It does not guarantee brotherhood and sisterhood. There is no correlation between knowledge and goodness. Benjamin Mays made this cogent observation:

> We use to believe, like Socrates, that evil and wrongdoing were based on ignorance; that men fought wars because they didn't know any better; that racial prejudice was based on a lack of knowledge; that man exploited man because he needed to be enlightened. But we know now that knowledge is not enough; that man can know the truth and deliberately lie, see the good and deliberately choose evil, see the light and deliberately walk in darkness, see the "high road" beckoning to him and deliberately choose the "low road."[2]

Having knowledge does not make a person do the good or moral thing in life. What we need is something that will dwell within us to give us power to apply knowledge and do good. This is why, when the devil tried to tempt a hungry Jesus to turn stones into bread, Jesus said, "Man shall not live by bread alone, but by every word that proceeds out of the mouth of God" (Matt 4:4, RSV). Jesus had the knowledge to turn bread into stones, but the Spirit within him gave him the power to resist the strong impulses of the flesh. After Jesus had resisted every temptation, Scripture points out, "Jesus returned in the power of the Spirit into Galilee, and a report concerning him went out through all the surrounding country" (Luke 4:14, RSV). It was the power of the Spirit and not knowledge alone that made Jesus effective.

The Spirit of the Lord

There are many demonic spirits in our world. They were present during the time of Jesus' ministry, and they are present today. They possessed people and caused them to harm themselves and others. But the Spirit of the Lord is greater and more powerful than all the evil and demonic spirits put together. This is why at the outset of his ministry Jesus said, "The Spirit of the Lord is upon me, because he has anointed me to preach good news to the poor. He has sent me to proclaim release to the captives and recovering of the sight to the blind, to set at liberty those who are oppressed, to proclaim the acceptable year of the Lord" (Luke 4:18-19, RSV). What makes us think that if Jesus depended on the Holy Spirit to lead, guide, and empower him during his earthly ministry, then we should not do the same? Without the aid and power of the Holy Spirit, Christianity would not have become a mainline world religion. Persecution could not stomp it out; heretics could not discredit it; scientists could not disprove it because the Holy Spirit has kept the work of Christ moving. Christopher Lasch wrote, "If there is one lesson we might have expected to learn in the 150 years . . . , it is that the schools can't save society. Crime and poverty are still with us, and the gap between rich and poor continues to widen."[3]

We Are Powerless without the Holy Spirit

Jesus said, "Without me you can do nothing." Literally, Jesus Christ means nothing. Without the Spirit of Christ or the Spirit of the Lord, we are powerless. James Forbes said, "It is understandable then why many burn out so soon. They have sought to do a spiritual task without the aid of the Spirit. This is not to deny the significance of human effort. On the contrary, human resources are highly valued and actually enriched by the anointing."[4] Jesus Christ is no longer with us physically, but he is with us through the Holy Spirit, and unless the Holy Spirit lives and dwells in us, we cannot do anything. We cannot stop the madness, insanity, and self-annihilation that have engulfed our civilization. We cannot beat back the nihilism that is so apparent in our cities, schools, and communities. We cannot inject hope and meaning in the veins of a dying culture unless. We cannot resurrect dry bones. Our crisis as a nation and world is a heart crisis, and no political party or legislation can change the hearts of people. The only thing that can change the hearts of people is the Holy Spirit, and once the heart is changed, character changes, then culture changes, and then customs change for the better.

Like the physical body cannot live long without water, we cannot live long without the Holy Spirit. We are dead as people, as a nation, and as a church without the Holy Spirit. Let us not fool ourselves; God sent us the Holy Spirit for a purpose. God is not an arbitrary or purposeless God. When we downplay, deny, or ignore the gift God sent us, we do so to our peril. Going into the world to make a difference for the kingdom of God without the Holy Spirit is like a soldier on the battlefield without a weapon. We must have the Holy Spirit if we are to be more than conquerors. This is the reason Paul encouraged the disciples, "Put on the whole armor of God, that you may be able to stand against the wiles of the devil . . . put on the breastplate of righteousness . . . the shield of faith . . . the helmet of salvation, and the sword of the Spirit, which is the word of God" (Eph 6:11, 14, 16-17, RSV). Without this armor, it would be different if not impossible to win this spiritual war. Our flesh is not enough to win it. Reconciliation and forgiveness between the races cannot be accomplished without the Holy Spirit. We are powerless without it.

The Holy Spirit at Work

Before his death, Jesus knew the disciples would scatter and desire to go back to their old lifestyles. He knew they could not keep the Christian movement going with their own strength. He knew the events of his crucifixion would strike fear in his disciples, and if the disciples did not quickly refocus, they would drift into irrelevance. Jesus promised to send them the Comforter, an aid that would not only empower them to do the work of the kingdom, but also give them the courage to speak truth to power. The Holy Spirit was their weapon in order to convict and convert, to wash and make people whole. Jesus promised that this powerful force would come to keep them moving during hostile times and sustain them through difficult situations. It was and is necessary for disciples to remain relevant.

We must understand that during New Testament times, the disciples were engaged in a cause so important to them that it demanded most of their time and energy. It demanded sacrifice; it demanded self-denial; it demanded bearing a cross. This cause put them in harm's way; for them it meant the loss of life and limb. It meant the loss of reputation. It was already rough following a leader who was considered a dangerous revolutionary, an agitator, a rabble-rouser, a troublemaker, and one who practiced civil disobedience and broke injunctions. It became tough when he was tried and convicted for treason, and even tougher when he was put to death. The crucifixion of Jesus crushed his disciples to the point that they did not want to struggle on. Many of them wanted to go back to their old professions. They didn't have the energy or the will power to carry on the movement Jesus started. The movement was making the religious and political leaders angry; it was changing people's worldview and perceptions of themselves. The old way was giving way for the new to take place. Even so, the disciples knew keeping this movement going would have deadly consequences. They met often in the upper room with the doors shut tight because they were too tired and afraid to go into the market places of society and be a witness for the man who had started this movement and preached the gospel of the kingdom of God. They knew they were few in number and that public opinion was against them. They knew they had no allies in the government and plenty of enemies among the religious establishment. It was a dangerous time for them, and with no charismatic leader to inspire them to carry on the struggle, these disciples found it difficult, if not impossible, to engage again in the movement to build the kingdom of God.

What was promised to them would be the same power that came upon Gideon, who was able to deliver God's people from their enemies. It would be the same power that came upon Samson, who was able to tear a lion apart and kill a thousand men in battle with a jawbone of an ass. It would be the same power that came upon David, who was able to take a slingshot and one stone and hit Goliath between the eyes, killing him instantly. It would be the same power that came upon the prophets, who were able to stand and say what God told them to say. The power of the Holy Spirit would work in and through the disciples to usher souls out of the kingdom of evil and into the kingdom of God.

When God sent the Holy Spirit, on a day we call Pentecost, the disciples were filled with the Spirit, and they began to speak with other tongues as the Spirit gave then utterance. These same frightened, closed-in disciples now boldly stood in the marketplaces preaching and witnessing for Jesus Christ.

After they were filled with the Holy Spirit, their fear turned into faith; their outlook turned into opportunities, their doubts turned into devotion; their religion turned into a revolution, and their problems turned into praise. They were a mighty force that turned the Greco-Roman world upside down. By the power of the Holy Spirit, the Christian movement convinced men and women in Caesar's house; it caused kings to tremble on their thrones and jailers to inquire what must they do to be saved.[5] Thousands joined the Christian movement because the Holy Spirit was at work in and through the believers. Many from the Roman Empire accepted Christ through the power of the Holy Spirit.

A Second Pentecost

The modern church has become cold and ineffective, slowly drifting into irrelevance. The reason for is that other things control the church instead of the Holy Spirit. When creeds, bylaws, committees, constitutions, and boards rule and run the church instead of the Holy Spirit, the church cannot be effective for the kingdom of God. Since Christ is the head of the church, whatever Christ says through the Holy Spirit should be adhered to without deviation. Revelation 1 and 2 reveal that Christ is speaking to the churches and beseeches those who have ears to hear what the Spirit says to the churches. When the church hears and obeys the Holy Spirit, divine power is released and Christ is glorified, the believers are edified, and the church multiplies. From the very day of Pentecost, the dominant personality in the early church was the Holy Spirit. Because the Holy Spirit directed and empowered the early church, thousands joined the church, did miracles, met needs, broke yokes, etc. If we want the same effect today, we must allow the Holy Spirit to rule and direct the church. The reason the early church was so powerful and effective is that they were a Holy Spirit-guided community of believers. Persecution and execution could not retard the Christian movement.

The apathy and complacency often found in the church is the direct result of the church operating without the Holy Spirit. Many church leaders are afraid to speak out against the social evils of our time. The church has become a priest to the status quo. The church has lost personalities like Martin Luther King Jr. who was not afraid to speak truth to power and create tension to encourage our nation to chart another course. Although the church has lost him and others, it has not lost the Holy Spirit. The Holy Spirit cannot be assassinated. It can be grieved, resisted, tempted, and lied to but never assassinated. Without the Holy Spirit, the modern church is like a treadmill; it is moving but going nowhere. The church is too quiet, too passive, and too lukewarm. It operates too much in the flesh and not enough in the power of the Holy Spirit. George O. McCalep Jr. wrote,

> Many in the church do not consider one of the purposes of the anointing as dismantling systems of oppression and evil power structures. They have not seen the obvious truth that we are to affect and change nations through the enabling power and ability of the Holy Ghost. We must be able to affect spirits or systems that control nations in order to disciple nations (Matthew 28:16-20).
>
> Much of the world, approximately eighty to ninety percent, is under a spirit or system of oppression, and because the truth of the anointing has not been fully realized, the church, in a large measure, has neither touched nor challenged these systems, but coexisted with them. . . . The church does not have many preachers who are brave enough and yielded enough to the Holy Ghost to speak out against the oppressor and his practice of controlling people. In fact, much of the church world benefits from the way things are and has no desire for things to change. Religion that aids present power structures also rejects and is intimidated by the anointing of the Spirit to deal with oppression. Anyone who ministers at a high level of the anointing of the Spirit and the truth of God's Word will be labeled a "radical" and "militant."[6]

Embarrassed by the Holy Spirit

The modern-day church seems embarrassed about the one thing God sent the disciples to use and depend on to advance the kingdom of God. The church has not utilized to the fullest, if at all, the power of the Holy Spirit, and therefore it is no wonder we have not been able to reduce or get rid of the staggering statistics facing us as a nation and community of faith. It is no wonder sin and discipline are downplayed and protected by the "cheap grace" we bestow on ourselves. It is no wonder we cannot tell the children of light from the children of darkness. It is no wonder we are not bothered by the sinful and wicked lifestyles of those in the pulpit and the pew. It is no wonder the problem of the color line is still within the church. We have become embarrassed by the Holy Spirit. The Holy Spirit is our power and our aid. It is amazing, as James Forbes put it that "Christians are Holy Spirit shy."

For some, conversations about empowerment of the Spirit in one's ministry are occasions of anxiety and intimidation. Some preachers hesitate to speak of the Spirit in relationship to what they do. Others talk about the Spirit in traditional language of faith, but without personal meaning. Hence, many of the biblical provisions for the Holy Spirit empowerment often are left unrealized like unclaimed packages or unopened letters.[7]

For the modern-day church to become relevant once again, we must not be shy about the Holy Spirit, but bold in allowing the Holy Spirit to use us in building the kingdom of God. The Holy Spirit was not sent to us to control it; it was sent to control and empower us in carrying out the will of God. Our land is in desperate need of Christian disciples who are full of the Holy Spirit. Too much is at stake for us to operate without its aid. Forbes wrote,

> Only by the anointing of the Spirit does the vision of God's Kingdom become so etched in the mind and heart that actions must flow from it. Only through anointed preachers will death and its structure of oppression be exposed for what they really are. Then guardians of that dominion can be set free from their self-strangulation and be brought to the fresh air of the wind of the Spirit. Only anointed preaching will make plain the truth, which makes transformation of life possible for both the oppressor and the oppressed.[8]

I have no doubt that the modern-day church needs a second Pentecost. We have relied too much on our own intelligence, our own strength, and our own way of life, and look where we are in human history. Look at the condition of our land. Look at the condition of the family, the community, the society, the youth, and the government. Every human institution is infected with the virus of decay. Our land is top heavy with division, injustice, oppression, corruption, and immorality. To inject life into the veins of our cultural decay, enough Christian disciples must be willing and unashamed to come under the power of the Holy Spirit and serve as instruments in the hands of God. James Forbes's assessment of our times is true: "Brothers and sisters, there's death in the land. There is death in ourselves, in our preaching, and in our institutions. But through the anointing power of the Holy Spirit, we must . . . cry out to God, 'Renew your people now!'"[9]

The Holy Spirit can and will renew us, but we must position ourselves by being in one accord, as were the early disciples, to receive it. Once we are filled with the Holy Spirit, we too shall experience a spiritual revolution and witness the transformation of lives and institutions in our nation and the world. We need the Holy Spirit to make the church what Christ envisioned it to be. The Holy Spirit quickens us not only to hear the word of the Lord, but it also empowers us to do something about wrong, evil, and injustice in our world. There is no doubt about it; we need the Holy Spirit to revive our souls again and give us power to carry out the mandates of the gospel so that we may build the kingdom of God in the twenty-first century.

Notes

1. Cited in Huston Smith, *World's Religions* (New York: HarperCollinsPublishers, 1994) 13.

2. Benjamin E. Mays, *Quotable Quotes* (New York: Vantage Press, 1983) 10.

3. Christopher Lasch, *The Revolt of the Elites and the Betrayal of Democracy* (New York: W. W. Norton & Company, 1995) 160.

4. James Forbes, *The Holy Spirit and Preaching* (Nashville: Abingdon Press, 1989) 50.

5. Martin Luther King Jr., *Strength to Love* (Philadelphia: Fortress Press, 1963) 104.

6. George O. McCalep Jr., *Sin in the House* (Lithonia GA: Orman Press, Inc., 1999) 150–51.

7. Forbes, *The Holy Spirit and Preaching*, 21–22.

8. Ibid., 88.

9. Ibid., 105.

Discussion Questions

1. This book speaks extensively to the need for black Americans to have education, economic power, and strong black leadership. In the final chapter, the author highlights the importance of the Holy Spirit in giving blacks the ability to apply their knowledge in positive ways. How do we know we have the Holy Spirit? How has the Holy Spirit moved in your personal life? In what ways can the church teach people to harness this spiritual source of power and inspiration?

_____

_____

_____

_____

2. Do you agree with the author's assessment that "demonic spirits" plague our world? Can you name examples of ways these spirits work in the lives of black people? How does one revoke the control such spirits have over his or her life?

_____

_____

_____

_____

3. The author discusses the danger of the disciples' path of following Jesus. They faced not only demonic spirits but also the governing authorities who wished to stifle Christianity, and the apathy of the people around them. How can following Jesus actually endanger your life, or at least your well-being? How does the disciples' example inspire you to work for positive changes in the black community in spite of the dangers?

_____

_____

_____

_____

4. The author writes that the "modern church has become cold and ineffective, slowly drifting into irrelevance." He says this is because things other
   than the Holy Spirit control the church. What controls the modern
   church? What would it take to redirect control to the Spirit? What would
   it take for the church to have a "second Pentecost"?

_____

_____

_____

_____

5. How optimistic are you when you assess the struggles of the black community? How committed are you, as a black person or as a person of
   another race, to improving the plight of other members of God's family?
   What practical steps can you take in your church and community to initiate change?

_____

_____

_____

_____

CONCLUSION

What to me is the multitude of your sacrifices? I have had enough of burnt offerings of rams and the fat of fed beasts; I do not delight in the blood of bulls or of lambs, or of goats. . . . Your new moons and your appointed festivals my soul hates . . . . Learn to do good; seek justice, rescue the oppressed, defend the orphan, plead for the widow.
—Isaiah 1:11, 14, 17, RSV

Relevant Once More

The foregoing analysis is my attempt to take a fresh look at the church and arouse its consciousness and action to get back to its origin. This is the only way it will survive and thrive in the twenty-first century. The church must again focus on serving and empowering the people so they can help change the economical, sociological, ecological, and political context in which they live. Without trained and Holy Spirit-filled people, black and white churches cannot fulfill their mission in the world. They cannot redeem the times in which we live. Only when the people of the world know that the church truly believes its own message of love, freedom, justice, and brotherhood and sisterhood will they respond to the gospel message and participate in carrying out the mandates of the gospel. Too often the creeds of the church have not met the deeds of the church. In many ways, the two are still mutually exclusive. However, to be relevant in the twenty-first century, the church must bring together its orthodoxy and orthopraxy. Today's church needs to work aggressively on becoming relevant again and helping people believe in the church and in themselves. When the church gets back to its original mission, we will see change in our world.

The Early Evangelical Movement

One cannot help being struck by the evangelical movement of the late eighteenth and early nineteenth centuries. This was a time in which the church was relevant with its Christian faith. We can learn much about this grassroots movement that brought significant changes to the Western world. The people at the bottom of the social heap were co-opted into the process of providing solutions to the social evils of the times, and this is the reason the evangelical movement was so effective. The outcasts, the marginalized, and the despised were made to feel that they were somebody and that they had something to offer in the transformation of society. The old theology of medieval Christendom that had often led to social quietism was replaced by an evangelical theology of social activism and service. The evangelical movement became an aggressive merging of the sacred and secular in an effort to change the theological, social, and political landscape for the transformation of the larger society. It put emphasis on a high sense of public duty to improve conditions in society and to struggle against structures that stifled transformation.

The church underwent a shift from traditional top-down forms of expression that dealt with liturgical rituals and strict moralism to expressions of love, forgiveness, repentance, and conversion. The evangelical movement put less emphasis on the transcendence of God and more emphasis on freedom, justice, equality, and repentance. Hope, equality, freedom, and renewal resonated with masses of people, making the evangelical movement the most powerful spiritual force in the Church of England and in America. Evangelical influence grew rapidly, and it insisted that the Bible and human conscience should be the primary frames of reference for authority. Supreme emphasis on the Bible was the major characteristic of evangelicalism. Adherents brought people back to the Bible and pointed out the common sin of humanity, the common dependence on God, and the common value of all God's people.[1] This theological posture brought hope to common people, the outcasts, the marginalized, the downtrodden, and the black slaves. The common people embraced evangelicalism favorably and aggressively, and they joined the movement not only to transform their personal lives but also to transform the social conditions in which they would live out their lives.

Instead of hearing theology from the top down, evangelical influence made it possible to hear theology from the bottom up. We can say that the evangelicals created a bottom-up view of reality and produced a bottom-up theology that put emphasis on the poor, the despondent, and the oppressed. If we are to reform society, it must be done from the bottom up in order to have lasting implications. Because of the great response of the people, these movements provided opportunities like never before for redemption, renewal, and equality. Laypeople were so empowered that they were instrumental in helping to push for social change. Even the rich were converted, and they started to practice accountability and stewardship and help provide for the needs of others in an effort to create a different world.[2.] The evangelicals of this period raised up a standard among the people by lifting high the Bible and its gospel of liberation that they believed was good news for the people, especially the poor, the brokenhearted, and those held captive by oppression. They were intentional about changing the social consciousness of their times. In their view, to uplift the downtrodden was a struggle to save England's soul.[3] Like England's was, I believe the soul of our nation is at stake, and we must create another spiritual movement like the evangelical movement of the late eighteenth and early nineteenth centuries.

The Civil Rights Movement

We saw a glimpse of the evangelical movement through the civil rights movement that also changed the social consciousness of the 1960s. Like the evangelical movement, the civil rights movement was a movement of agitation that radically changed the social order. Leaders like Martin Luther King Jr. were loving in their confrontation with powers. Our next spiritual movement needs loving leaders of all races to build a coalition to help save the nation. Movements are necessary for a nation headed for destruction. I believe serious Christians must not stand on the sideline and watch the demise of the nation. To turn our nation around from its destructive path, we need another spiritual movement to combat our narcissistic culture. We don't need more churches but a movement to change social consciousness and create again a culture of social responsibility, civic duty, and accountability. Without a movement to struggle for the Christian values and principles that made our nation great, America stands on the threshold of reproach not only before God but also before the nations of the world.

President Barack Obama and the Concept of Change

It is exciting that President Barack Obama is the first African-American president of the United States. People of every faith, race, class, and gender came together to elect this young charismatic leader who ran a campaign promising change. When Obama was sworn in as president, I concluded that America is maturing, judging the content of character instead of the color of a person's skin. President Barack Obama is a product of the dream of Martin Luther King Jr. He is an intelligent and well-qualified person to lead the country. Although I am happy and elated about this historic election of the first black president, I am wise enough to know that President Obama cannot do more for a people than they are willing to do for themselves. President Obama represents hope for millions of people, especially black people, but at the same time he does not have a magic wand to wave to make the problems of the nation and the black community disappear. The change President Obama promises to make will not dramatically change the crisis within black America. Black America still suffers from economic, social, and political oppression, and to help oppressed people, the social and economic system in which the oppressed live must be corrected. In other words, the system's playing field must be leveled; otherwise, the change President Obama promised to make is nothing more than a different face with the same body politic. Unless the system is radically corrected, we can expect the same unequal distribution of power and access.

The American system has undergone a change but not a correction. The white house now has a different face, but until there is a fundamental correction of the system, there will continue to be a wide gap between the rich and the poor, the haves and the have-nots. This is not an indictment against President Obama. He is not the problem. Oppression is the problem.

Black America must not expect President Obama to be their salvation. It is a good thing to have allies in the government to help a people in their quest for liberation and self-sufficiency, but allies cannot do for a people what they can do for themselves. We should know this by now because we have more elected black officials than ever before, and black Americans still suffer and top the list in many detrimental social, economic, and educational statistics. Let us not fall into the fantasy that all is well for the future now that President Obama leads America. If we look back in history, we will currently experience déjà vu. Lerone Bennett wrote an article titled "The Second Reconstruction: Is History Repeating Itself?" The essence of the article was that black people made significant social and political progress and lost it. In his introduction he wrote,

> Over.
>
> It was, at long last, over and done with. How could anyone doubt it? How could anyone fail to see that the race problem had been solved forever?
>
> One man who had no doubt said, "All distinctions founded upon race or color have been forever abolished in the United States."
>
> Another who saw things this way said the category of race has been abolished by law and that "there" [were] no more colored people in this country."
>
> Thus spoke the dreamers and the prophets—and victims in the first Reconstruction of the 1860s and the 1870s. . . .
>
> And it is worth emphasizing here, at the very beginning, that these flights into fantasy were based on the same "hard" facts that grip the imagination of Blacks in the second Reconstruction of the 1960s and 1970s. There was, for example, a Black man in the U.S. Senate in the 1870s and there was a Black governor in Louisiana. In the 1860s and the 1870s—as in the 1960s and 1970s—there were Black sheriffs and mayors in the South and there was open speculation about a Black vice presidential candidate.[4]

We see that the gains black people made in the 1860s and 1870s were lost, and it took another 100 years of tears and struggle to regain it. Although laws are on the books, they are no stronger than their enforcers. The people who make the laws must enforce them, and if they change their minds about a people, then those laws have no power.[5]

Black people cannot put their trust and liberation in the hands of the government. It is better for a people to own and control their own institutions, so they can send their own politicians to protect their interests. Black people are still trying to create a political base before an economic base. We have not yet learned that economics drives everything else. Why is it we don't see any Koreans in Congress or in the Senate, yet they own and control 90 percent of the fruit and vegetable stores? Why don't we find Chinese people in Congress or in the Senate, but yet they own and control all the Chinese restaurants in the nation? They have thrived so that they have Chinatowns across the nations. Why don't we see Indian people in Congress or in the Senate, but yet they own service stations all across this country?

These groups understand solidarity as a way to ensure their survival. They are not trying to build a political base before an economic base.

Black people are still victims of miseducation. We still think and operate individually instead of collectively, and this is why having President Obama in the Oval Office will not move us up the social and economic ladder. Carter G. Woodson reminded us that "those who have not learned to do for themselves and have to depend solely on others never obtain any more rights or privileges in the end than they had in the beginning. . . . The race has great possibilities. Properly awakened, the Negro can do the so-called impossible in the business world and thus help to govern rather than merely be governed."[6] President Obama can be our ally but never our solution. Our solution can only come from within us. We must do our part and help create a new nation where all of us can take ownership of the blessings of freedom.

We Must Struggle Again

To get results, we must struggle again. Frederick Douglass made a profound statement: "If there is no struggle there is no progress. Those who profess to favor freedom and yet depreciate agitation, are men who want crops without plowing up the ground, they want rain without thunder and lightning. They want the ocean without the awful roar of its many waters."[7] History shows us that social transformation cannot be left to chance. There must be a call to action to change the present situation. To change society, the church must be willing to change, and internal change can influence external change. The church must become service-oriented again. This doesn't mean the church should assist people to be helpless, but empower the people so the people can help themselves. Too many people have a social psychology of dependence that keeps them helpless and codependent on others to do for them what they can do for themselves. To empower the people means to help them break from codependence to learn how to be interdependent. Interdependence is a community mutually dependent on each other. The early Christians of the first century were mutually dependent on one another. They struggled together. There was no "learned helplessness" among them. They all contributed in one way or another to build a Christian community. Because the early Christians shared what they had, there was no needy among them. Acts 4:32-35, NIV, says,

> All the believers were one in heart and mind. No one claimed that any of his possessions was his own, but they shared everything they had. With

great power the apostles continued to testify to the resurrection of the Lord Jesus, and much grace was upon them all. There were no needy persons among them. For from time to time those who owned lands or houses sold them, brought the money from the sales and put it at the apostles' feet, and it was distributed to anyone as he had need.

This is a clear example of how the early Christian believers assisted one another through a remarkable display of unity and service toward one another. They understood that they were their brothers' and sisters' keepers, and if the community of faith would not keep their brothers and sisters, who would? For the church to be relevant in the twenty-first century, it must get back to giving service, empowering the people, and struggling against unjust and unfair institutions. The church can no longer practice selfishness and have an "I got mine and you get yours" mentally. Dr. Kenneth Smith made this observation for the future of the black church:

> In the new century, the Black church's strength and presence will depend upon its leadership's capacity to be caregivers. The church must be a drum major for justice, and an advocate for the "least of these" among us. The Black church's strength and presence will also depend upon the capacity of the church to be a place where people feel empowered to discuss all community issues, explore all of the community's pain and then fashion a promise for the community.
>
> Its strength and presence will depend upon its capacity to develop educational programs for young people and adults alike which focus on heritage, self-affirmation, human sexuality, what it means to be a man or woman, health, and biblical principles.
>
> The Black church's strengths and presence will depend upon whether the army of volunteers housed in every church will be able to move beyond individual religious approaches to a communal religious response. This means moving from bench membership to embracing young men and women and becoming role models and mentors for them. How will children know if someone does not show them? If not now, when? If not us, who?[8]

Black and white churches are faced with a choice either to be relevant or irrelevant in the twenty-first century. The salvation of generations to come will depend on our decision today. It is my hope that we chose to be relevant instead of irrelevant as members in the Body of Christ.

Notes

1. Mark A. Noll, *America's God* (New York: Oxford University Press, 2002) 161.

2. Ibid., 10.

3. Ibid.

4. Cited from Amos N. Wilson, *The Falsification of Afrikan Consciousness* (New York: Afrikan World InfoSystems, 1993) 9–10.

5. Ibid., 10.

6. Carter G. Woodson, *Miseducation of the Negro* (Washington DC: The Associated Publishers: 1969) 186–87.

7. John Blassingame, *The Frederick Douglass Papers*, "Speeches, Debates, and Interviews, 1855–1863," series 3, vol. 3 (New Haven: Yale University Press, 1985) 204.

8. *Biblical Strategies for a Community in Crisis: What African Americans Can Do*, ed. Colleen Birchett (Chicago: Urban Ministries, Inc., 1992) 204.

BIBLIOGRAPHY

Books

Akbar, Naim. *Breaking the Chains of Psychological Slavery.* Tallahassee: Mind Productions & Associates, 1996.

————. *Know Thy Self.* Tallahassee: Mind Productions & Associates, 1998.

Ali, Carroll A. Watkins. *Survival and Liberation Pastoral Theology in African American Context.* St. Louis: Chalice Press, 1999.

Baer, Hans A., and Merrill Singer. *African American Religion in the Twentieth Century.* Knoxville: University of Tennessee Press, 1992.

Barclay, William. *The Gospel of John.* Volume 2. Philadelphia: Westminster Press, 1956.

Barndt, Joseph. *Dismantling Racism: The Continuing Challenge to White America.* Minneapolis: Augsburg Press, 1991.

Bell, Janet Cheatham. *Famous Black Quotations.* Chicago: Sabayt Publications, 1986.

Bellah, Robert N. *The Good Society.* New York: Vintage Books, 1992.

Bennett, Lerone Jr. *The Challenge of Blackness.* Chicago: Johnson Publishing Company, 1972.

Benson-Hale, Janice. *Working with Black Youth: Opportunities for Christian Ministry,* edited by Charles R. Foster and Grant S. Shockley. Nashville: Abingdon Press, 1989.

Birchett, Colleen, editor. *Biblical Strategies for a Community in Crisis: What African Americans Can Do.* Chicago: Urban Ministries, Inc., 1992.

Blassingame, John. *The Frederick Douglass Papers.* "Speeches, Debates, and Interviews." Series 3. Volume 3. New Haven: Yale University Press, 1985.

Bonhoeffer, Dietrich. *The Cost of Discipleship.* New York: Macmillan Publishing Company, 1963.

Cleage, Albert B. *The Black Messiah.* New Jersey: Africa World Press, Inc., 1995.

Cone, James H. *A Black Theology of Liberation.* New York: Orbis Books, 1986.

———. *Black Theology and Black Power.* New York: Orbis Books, 1997.

———. *For My People.* New York: Orbis Books, 1984.

———. *Speaking the Truth.* New York: Orbis Books, 1999.

Cose, Ellis. *The Rage of a Privileged Class.* New York: HarperCollins Publishers, Inc., 1993.

———. *The Envy of the World.* New York: Washington Square Press, 2002.

Douglass, Frederick. *Life and Times of Frederick Douglass.* New York: Macmillan Publishing Company, 1962.

Du Bois, W. E. B. *The Souls of Black Folk.* New York: NAL Penguin, Inc., 1969.

Dyson, Michael Eric. *Can You Hear Me Now?* New York: Basic Civitas Books, 2009.

Ellison, Ralph. *Invisible Man.* New York: Random House, 1947.

Felder, Cain Hope. *Troubling Biblical Waters.* New York: Orbis Books, 1989.

Foluke, Gyasi A. *The Real Holocaust: A Wholistic Analysis of the African-American Experience 1441–1994.* New York: Carlton Press Corporation, 1995.

Foner, Philip S. *The Life and Writings of Frederick Douglass.* Volume 2. New York: International Publishers, 1950–1975.

Forbes, James. *The Holy Spirit & Preaching.* Nashville: Abingdon Press, 1989.

Forell, George W. *Christian Social Teaching.* Minneapolis: Augsburg Publishing House, 1966.

Fountain, Ernest M. *To Achieve the American Dream.* Las Vegas: Fountain Financial Services LLC, 2000.

Frazier, E. Franklin. *The Negro Church in America.* New York: Schocken Books, 1974.

———. *Black Bourgeoisie.* New York: Collier Books, 1965.

Freire, Paulo. *Pedagogy of the Oppressed.* New York: Continuum Publishing Company, 1999.

Hacker, Andrew. *Two Nations Black and White, Separate, Hostile, Unequal.* New York: Ballantine Books, 1992, 1995.

Hinchliff, Peter. *Holiness and Politics.* Grand Rapids: William B. Eerdmans Publishing Company, 1982.

Johnson, John L. *The Black Biblical Heritage.* St. Louis MO: Black Biblical Heritage Publishing Company, 1988.

Jones, Amos Jr. *Paul's Message of Freedom: What Does It Means to the Black Church.* Valley Forge PA: Judson Press, 1984.

King, Martin Luther Jr. *Where Do We Go From Here: Chaos or Community?* New York: Harper and Row, 1967.

———. *Strength to Love.* Philadelphia: Fortress Press, 1963.

Lasch, Christopher. *The Revolt of the Elites and the Betrayal of Democracy.* New York: W. W. Norton & Company, 1995.

C. Eric Lincoln and Laurence H. Mamiya. *The Black Church in the African American History.* Durham NC: Duke University Press, 1990.

Loeb, Paul Rogat. *Soul of a Citizen.* New York: St. Martin's Press, 1999.

Mays, Benjamin E. *Quotable Quotes.* New York: Vantage Press, 1983.

———. *The Negro's God.* New York: Atheneum, 1969.

McCalep, George O. Jr. *Sin in the House.* Lithonia GA: Orman Press, Inc., 1999.

Niebuhr, Richard H. *The Social Sources of Denominationalism.* New York: The World Publishing Company, 1957.

Quarles, Benjamin. *Black Abolitionists.* New York: Oxford University Press, 1969.

Raboteau, Albert J. *Slave Religion.* New York: Oxford University Press, 1978.

Sernett, Milton C. *Afro-American Religious History A Documentary Witness.* Durham NC: Duke University Press, 1985.

Smith, Huston. *World's Religions.* New York: HarperCollins Publishers, 1994.

Snowden, Frank M. *Before Color Prejudice.* Cambridge MA: Harvard University Press, 1983.

―――. *Blacks in Antiquity.* Cambridge MA: Harvard University Press, 1970.

Thurman, Howard. *The Luminous Darkness.* Richmond IN: Friends United Press, 1989.

―――. *Deep River and The Negro Spiritual Speaks of Life and Death.* Richmond IN: Friends United Press, 1975.

―――. *Disciplines of the Spirit.* Richmond IN: Friends United Press, 1987.

Walker, Daniel D. *The Human Problems of the Minister.* New York: Harper & Row Publishers, 1960.

Warren, Rick. *The Purpose Driven Church.* Grand Rapids MI: Zondervan Publishing Co., 1995.

Washington, James Melvin, editor. *A Testament of Hope.* San Francisco: Harper & Row Publishers, 1986.

Watson, Lillian E., editor. *Light from Many Lamps.* New York: Simon & Schuster, 1951.

Wentzel, Fred D. *Epistle to White Christians.* Philadelphia: The Christian Education Press, 1948.

West, Cornel. *Race Matters.* New York: Vintage Book, 1993.

―――. *Prophetic Reflections Notes on Race and Power in America.* Monroe ME: Common Courage Press, 1993.

Williams, Juan. *Enough: The Phony Leaders, Dead-End Movements, and Culture of Failure that Are Undermining Black America—and What We Can Do About It.* New York: Three Rivers Press, 2006.

Wilmore, Gayraud S. *Black Religion and Black Radicalism: An Interpretation of the Religious History of Afro-American People.* New York: Orbis Books, 1983.

―――. *Black Theology A Documentary History, 1966–1979.* New York: Orbis Books, 1979.

Wilson, Amos N. *Blueprint for Black Power A Moral, Political and Economic Imperative for the Twenty-First Century.* New York: Afrikan World Infosystem, 1998.

―――. *Awakening the Natural Genius of Black Children.* New York: Afrikan World InfoSystems, 1991.

———. *The Falsification of Afrikan Consciousness.* New York: Afrikan World InfoSystem, 1993.

Woodson, Carter G. *Miseducation of the Negro.* Washington DC: The Associated Publishers, Inc. 1933, 1969.

———. *Negro Orators and their Orations.* Washington DC: Associated Publishers, 1925.

Articles and Essays

Brown, Lamarr. "Is There an Economic War on Black America?" *New Journal & Guide* (Norfolk VA), 26 October 2005.

Copher, Charles B. "Three Thousand Years of Biblical Interpretation with Reference to Black People." *Journal of the Interdenominational Theological Center* 30/2 (Spring 1986).

Gala, Larry (professor of History and Government at Wilmington College). "Brilliant Thoughts and Important Truth: A Speech of Frederick Douglass," 1852.

Humphrey, Jeffrey M. "The Multicultural Economy 2003 America's Minority Buying Power." *Georgia Business and Economic Conditions* 63/2 (Second Quarter 2003).

Jones, William R. "The Religious Legitimation of Counterviolence: Insights from Latin America Liberation Theology." In Lonnie D. Kliever, editor, *The Terrible Meek: Revolution and Religion in Cross-cultural Perspective.* New York: Paragon Press, 1987.

———. "Purpose and Method in Liberation Theology: Implication for an Interim Assessment." *Liberation Theology: North American Style*, edited by Deane William Ferm. New York: International Religious Foundation, 1987.

———. "The Arts in the Community: Toward a Deeper Understanding of Black Aesthetics." Unpublished manuscript.

Noll, Mark A. *America's God.* New York: Oxford University Press, 2002.

The Report of the National Advisory Commission on Civil Disorder, US Government Printing Office, 1968.